100 THINGS TO DO IN CHARLOTTE BEFORE YOU DIE

View of the Uptown skyline from South End. Photo by Andy Weber

100 THINGS TO DO IN CHARLOTTE BEFORE YOU DIE

3rd Edition

BRIANNA CRANE

REEDY PRESS

Copyright © 2024 by Reedy Press, LLC
Reedy Press
PO Box 5131
St. Louis, MO 63139, USA
reedypress.com

No part of this publication may be reproduced or transmitted in any form or by any means, electronic or mechanical, including photocopy, recording, or any information storage and retrieval system, without permission in writing from the publisher.

Permissions may be sought directly from Reedy Press at the above mailing address or via our website at reedypress.com.

Library of Congress Control Number: 2024938916

ISBN: 9781681065342

Unless otherwise noted, all photos are courtesy of the author or believed to be in the public domain. Author headshot photo courtesy of Ramsey Yanney.

Design by Jill Halpin

Printed in the United States of America
24 25 26 27 28   5 4 3 2

We (the publisher and the author) have done our best to provide the most accurate information available when this book was completed. However, we make no warranty, guarantee, or promise about the accuracy, completeness, or currency of the information provided, and we expressly disclaim all warranties, express or implied. Please note that attractions, company names, addresses, websites, and phone numbers are subject to change or closure, and this is outside of our control. We are not responsible for any loss, damage, injury, or inconvenience that may occur due to the use of this book. When exploring new destinations, please do your homework before you go. You are responsible for your own safety and health when using this book.

DEDICATION

To my granny, Dixie Sue Woodbury. She always indulged my curiosity, and we played tourist in our town of Wilmington more days than I can count. She would have really loved this.

CONTENTS

Acknowledgments xiii
Preface xiv

Food and Drink

  1. Do Date Night at Stagioni 2
  2. Eat Traditional African Food at Abugida Ethiopian Cafe 4
  3. Get Your Chicken Fix at Bojangles 5
  4. Sample Your Way through Optimist Hall 6
  5. Savor Southern Cuisine at Leah & Louise 7
  6. Satisfy Your Burger Craving at Rusty's Deli & Grille 8
  7. Have One (or Two) Scoops from Two Scoops 9
  8. Get an Oatmeal Creme Pie from The Batch House 10
  9. Taste Your Way through Charlotte's Thai Scene Starting at Basil Thai 12
  10. Do Brunch at El Puro Cuban Restaurant 14
  11. Dine at RH Rooftop Restaurant 15
  12. Build Your Own Charcuterie Box from Babe & Butcher 16
  13. Celebrate Something Special at Kindred 17
  14. Sip Mezcal from Puerta 18
  15. Do a Nonalcoholic Pairing at Restaurant Constance 20

16. Slurp Transfusions on Selwyn Avenue Pub's Patio 21

17. Have a Classic Steak Dinner at Beef 'N Bottle 22

18. Sip Sangria at Noda Company Store 23

19. Cure Your Indian Food Craving at Curry Gate 24

20. Do a Group Dinner (or Lunch) at Calle Sol 26

21. Stroll through Rosie's Coffee & Wine Garden 27

22. Indulge in a Dulce de Leche Latte at Sumaq Coffee 28

23. Hop between Breweries in South End 30

24. Get a Taste of the Low Country at Mert's Heart and Soul 32

25. Grab a Sandwich and a Beer From the Common Market 33

26. Order Lunch from Pasta & Provisions 34

27. Have Happy Hour at Dilworth Tasting Room 35

28. Recharge at The Pauline Tea-Bar Apothecary 36

29. Crush a Crab Cake from Lulu's 37

30. Light Up All Five Senses at Counter- 38

31. Venture into Vegan at Oh My Soul 39

32. Get Cozy at Customshop 40

33. Trust the Lang Van Hype 41

34. Watch an FC Match at Salud Cerveceria 42

35. Say Yes to Yuca Balls at Yunta 43

36. Do Dinner at Al Mike's 44

37. Dine in a Beautifully Restored Church at Supperland 45

38. Taste Every Taco in Town, Starting at Noche Bruta 46

Music and Entertainment

39. Find Creativity and Community at Camp North End 50

40. Riff through Records at Lunchbox 51

41. Let Live Music Move You 52

42. Enjoy a Show at the Comedy Zone 53

43. Catch a Concert at BoFA 54

44. See a Broadway Show at Blumenthal 56

45. Take a Self-Guided Mural Tour 57

46. Celebrate Art at Charlotte SHOUT! 58

47. Roll the Dice at Luck Factory Games 59

48. Make a Candle at Paddywax Candle Bar 60

49. Stroll through SOCO 61

50. Dance the Night Away at the Music Yard 62

51. Find Your New Favorite Book at Park Road Books 63

52. See a Live Show at the Neighborhood Theatre 64

53. Have a Sophisticated Night Out at Middle C Jazz 65

Sports and Recreation

54. Get Your Steps In at the Rail Trail 68

55. Unleash Your Inner Adventurer at the US National Whitewater Center 69

56. Play Pickleball at Rally 70

57. Hike Crowders Mountain 71

58. Make New Friends (and Get a Little Exercise) at Mad Miles
    Run Club.. 72

59. Cheer On Our Hometown Teams.. 74

60. Make a Bouquet at Mclawland Farms 75

61. Head to Mood House for the Ultimate Self-Care Solo Date 76

62. People-Watch at the Wells Fargo Championship 77

63. Glide into the Holiday Spirit with Ice-Skating
    at the Whitewater Center.. 78

64. Get Your Adrenaline Pumping at Carowinds 80

65. Hike along a Greenway 81

66. Take an Epic Weekend Getaway to Charleston 82

67. Put Those Imaginary Golf Swings to Good Use at Puttery................ 84

68. Paddle on the Catawba.. 86

69. Explore Seven Oaks Nature Preserve 87

70. Pick Your Produce from a Farmers Market 88

Culture and History

71. Place Your Annual Baklava Sundae Order at the Greek Fest 92

72. Buy Local Art at BlkMrktClt... 93

73. Play Art Critic at The Mint 94

74. Take the Kiddos to the Great Elizabeth Pumpkin Wall..................... 96

75. Celebrate Black Culture and Coffee at Archive CLT 97

76. Taste Bites by Black Chefs... 98

77. Get Your Turkey Leg Fix at Carolina Renaissance Festival 99

x

78. Discover Something New with the Family 100

79. Get into the Holiday Spirit at the Southern Christmas Show 102

80. Let the Lights Dazzle You at Christmas Town U.S.A. 103

81. Celebrate Pride Month . . . in August 104

82. Take a Culinary Road Trip to Jon G's 105

83. Experience Afternoon Tea at Chez Marie Pâtisserie 106

84. Soak In Charlotte History in Uptown 107

85. Cook Up Some Fun with Chef Alyssa 108

86. Find Nonalc Community with Counterculture Club 109

Shopping and Fashion

87. Peruse the Provisions at Reid's Fine Foods 112

88. Hunt for Home Decor at House of Nomad 113

89. Score Secondhand Designer Fashions at the EDIT Sale 114

90. Find Something Funky at Thrift Pony 116

91. Shop 'Til You Drop at Phillips Place 118

92. Get Lost in Sleepy Poet 120

93. Find Curvy Couture at Juicy Body Goddess 121

94. Procure the Perfect Present from Paper Skyscraper 122

95. Tap into Your Craft at Curio, Craft & Conjure 124

96. Meander through Atherton Mill 125

97. Stroll around SouthPark Mall 126

98. Pick a Plant from Oakdale Greenhouses 127

99. Treat Yourself to a Treasure From Tiny Gods Jewelry Store **128**

100. Buy Something Stylish and Special at Thirty-One Jane **130**

Activities by Season **131**

Suggested Itineraries **135**

Index **137**

ACKNOWLEDGMENTS

Thank you to my husband, TJ. You're my favorite person to explore any city with, including our own. Your patience, support, and steady love give me the courage to do things that scare me, like write a book.

Thank you to my Axios Charlotte/Charlotte Agenda family. I wouldn't know and love this city like I do without you. No one cheers harder for Charlotte than you wonderful people. Special thanks to Emma Way for gut-checking me along the way, and to Andy Weber for graciously sharing his photos.

And last but never least, thanks to my parents who always knew my name would be on shelves one day. Your belief in me powers me more than you know.

PREFACE

Since the last version of this guidebook was written by the formidable Sarah Crosland, our city has added so many treasures to its trove, including a professional soccer team. We've also lost good ones along the way, perhaps making way for the new, but this new chapter deserves a new book. It's time to celebrate our resilience, natural beauty, and close-knit community of creatives.

Believe it or not, narrowing this list down to 100 things to do was quite the challenge. Charlotte's brimming with bucket-list worthy to-dos. This isn't a comprehensive guide to everything great Charlotte has to offer. Rather, *100 Things to Do in Charlotte Before You Die* is a starting point, intended to capture the spirit of what makes this place special.

If you're just visiting, I hope you leave Charlotte having tried something you can't or wouldn't normally try at home. I also hope you run by Bojangles to buy your own personal shaker of seasoning. Sprinkle it on your fries every time you miss us.

If you're new to town, I hope *100 Things to Do in Charlotte Before You Die* makes this city quickly feel like home. And if you're a native, I hope you're inspired to rediscover an old favorite or spend time adventuring in a new-to-you part of town.

No matter how long you're here for, take time to get to know the people. Our city has a lot that's shiny and new—and I'm grateful to live in a place that's willing to experiment and expand—but the city is steeped in decades-long cultural history, too. People make history, people push us forward, and in Charlotte, they do it with kindness and care. Writing this book I was reminded that if you embrace Charlotte, it'll embrace you right back.

The bar at Supperland

FOOD AND DRINK

DO DATE NIGHT
AT STAGIONI

This cozy, contemporary Italian restaurant, owned by Chef Bruce Moffett, is an idyllic choice for any date night or celebration. With minimal lighting and an intimate dining room, everyone glows in the tabletop candlelight, and whatever music might be playing is hushed by buzzy conversations.

Stagioni keeps a tight menu that rotates seasonally—from peach-topped pizzas in summer to creamy butternut squash soup in fall—so it's best to sample your way through each section and order to share. The calamari Caesar salad, meatballs, and pizza are must-order menu staples. The pizzas, which are delightfully crispy and topped with fresh mozzarella, are served with scissors so you can cut your own slice.

The New England chef also owns Good Food on Montford, Barrington's, and Bao and Broth—all indelible pieces of Charlotte's culinary scene worthy of your time.

715 Providence Rd., 704-372-8110
stagioniclt.com

SOME OTHER CROWD FAVORITES

Oggi
Best for those nights you want a modern, classic Italian joint.
16646 Hawfield Way Dr., 704-716-9400
oggicharlotte.com

Mama Ricotta's
Best for comforting, homestyle classics.
601 S Kings Dr. AA, 704-343-0148
mamaricottas.com

Little Mama's
Best for warm mounds of mozzarella and cocktails.
4521 Sharon Rd., 980-209-0323
9825 Sandy Rock Pl., Ste. 1A, 704-520-3601
littlemamasitalian.com

Aqua e Vino
Best for a romantic date night.
4219 Providence Rd., Ste. 3, 704-364-4445
aquaevino.com

Ever Andalo
Best for a double date or group dinner.
3116 N Davidson St., 704-910-6543
everandalo.com

Portofino's
Best for a massive pizza.
multiple locations
portofinos-us.com

Osteria Luca
Best for a lunch deal—and really good bread pudding.
4127 Park Rd., 704-910-0142
osterialuca.com

EAT TRADITIONAL AFRICAN FOOD
AT ABUGIDA ETHIOPIAN CAFE

Whether you're new to African cuisine or grew up on it, Abugida Ethiopian Cafe & Restaurant won't disappoint. And if you are new to the cuisine, their welcoming staff will guide you through the menu. This family-run spot, created by mother-daughter duo Shito and Yodite, has been around since 2016. But all of the recipes are generations-old family creations that predate this well-loved Central Avenue staple.

You can expect Ethiopian classics like sambusas, kitfo, zelzel wet, and beef tibs. If you want to taste your way through a large portion of the menu, consider the Abugida Feast, which comes with chicken or beef and all of the vegetable sides (except shiro) and a salad. There are plenty of vegetarian, vegan, and gluten-free dishes to choose from, too. Either way, be sure to experience the Ethiopian coffee ceremony, which promises a delightful combination of a strong coffee and energy-clearing incense.

3007 Central Ave., 980-237-2760
abugidacafe.com

GET YOUR CHICKEN FIX
AT BOJANGLES

Where you get your fried chicken is a personal choice, but Bojangles has been making that choice a little easier since 1977. It's hard to believe the widespread fast-casual joint had its humble beginnings right on West Boulevard. It's the place to order Cajun filet biscuits and Bo rounds by morning, or a Bo berry biscuit if you want something sweet. Try the supremes for supper, and ask for a little extra seasoning no matter the time of day.

You can order your own shaker of that special seasoning at most locations. It makes the perfect souvenir, or if you're local, grab a few for crowd-favorite stocking stuffers and your own spice rack. Luckily, if you are visiting and a Bojangles run doesn't fit into your itinerary, there's a location in the airport you can stop by on your way out.

multiple locations
bojangles.com

SAMPLE YOUR WAY THROUGH OPTIMIST HALL

When I'm trying to appease a pack of picky eaters, Optimist Hall is always the answer. Bao buns, burgers, barbecue—there's a little something for everyone at this airy, industrial food hall.

I suggest you start your quest at the Dumpling Lady, a family-run Sichuan restaurant that began as a farmers market booth before blossoming into a popular food truck in 2016. Now, the Dumpling Lady has a stall at Optimist Hall and a restaurant in South End. The Optimist Hall location is tried-and-true to the original food truck menu, focused on dumplings and noodles.

Try Asian street food from Bao and Broth. Eat something Ethiopian from Enat. Split a grilled cheese from Papi Queso. Feast on a fried chicken sandwich from Boxcar Betty's. Or sample some barbecue from Noble Smoke, one of Charlotte's favorite pulled pork purveyors.

1115 N Brevard St.
optimisthall.com

5

SAVOR SOUTHERN CUISINE
AT LEAH & LOUISE

River chips, squash grits, and creative sips—that's a small taste of the Mississippi-inspired dishes to pick from at Leah & Louise, a modern juke joint run by Chef Greg Collier and his wife, Subrina Collier. The Southern eatery earned its permanent place in Charlotte culinary history when Greg became the first chef in Charlotte to advance past the semifinalist round in the James Beard Foundation awards.

As soon as you step into Leah & Louise, the storytelling begins. A community table sits in the middle of the restaurant, and notes from the jukebox fill the air. The Colliers infuse their heritage and family origin stories into each dish with a special amount of care that makes the simplest dishes delightful. Take Leah's Cabbage, the dish on everyone's lips: a humble cabbage, slow-roasted with pepper honey, smoked sausage, and a pork neck bisque base.

980-309-0690
leahandlouise.com

TIP

Charlotte can't get enough of this iconic restaurant so they're relocating to a bigger space. Find reopening details at leahandlouise.com

SATISFY YOUR BURGER CRAVING
AT RUSTY'S DELI & GRILLE

This no-frills burger joint has been cooking up American classics for more than 40 years. It's not flashy. You get crispy fries, Styrofoam cups, and entrées served on plastic trays. It's simple and reliably good. It's in the name so you can trust the burger is worth ordering. The sesame-seed bun, ooey-gooey cheese, somehow-always-ripe tomatoes, subtly sweet grilled onions, and one juicy patty always hits the spot. But if you have a hankering for a different kind of sandwich, go with the chicken Philly or a triple-decker, bacon-loaded Carolina club. No matter what you order, don't skip a little ranch for those fries. Fun fact: my husband, who grew up in Charlotte, introduced me to Rusty's years ago, and we've been known to spend a Valentine's Day or two here.

8512 Park Rd., 704-554-9012
rustysdeli.com

HAVE ONE (OR TWO) SCOOPS
FROM TWO SCOOPS

Two Scoops Creamery gets two thumbs up from me, and it's one of my favorite treats in town. The local ice cream shop was opened by three best friends in 2016. Since the scoop shop's beginnings in Plaza Midwood, the trio has added several other locations across the Charlotte region. No matter where you stop in, you can count on a solid mix of classic and over-the-top offerings.

Cake batter lovers should try Krazy Kake—a vanilla-based ice cream with chunks of yellow cake and sprinkles (or Chocolate Krazier Kake, a chocolate-based version). If it's on the menu, and you want something even more creative, go with Why So Cereal?—a cereal-flavored ice cream with Lucky Charms marshmallows, Fruity Pebbles, and Crunch Berries. Looking for something classic? Go with the soft-serve.

913 Central Ave., 704-900-5792
1616 Camden Rd., Ste.100, 980-237-2149
119 Landings Dr., Ste. 104, Mooresville, 980-444-3800
161 W Main St., Ste. 102, Rock Hill, SC, 704-413-7646
twoscoopscreamery.com

GET AN OATMEAL CREME PIE
FROM THE BATCH HOUSE

In 2020, a record-breaking flood forced the original Batch House to close. The shop had only been open for about a year, but the beloved bakery had already won over Charlotteans who begged owner Cris Rojas Agurcia to open another spot. It took 11 months for Cris and her small-but-mighty crew to find and open a new location—and it was well worth the wait.

The perfectly pink bakery is decked out in granny chic decor, with cutouts of Blanche, Rose, Dorothy, and Sophia, a not-so-subtle homage to Cris's love for The Golden Girls. The oatmeal creme pie is one of the Batch House's signature items, but other menu highlights include s'mores brownies, cake pints, and chocolate puddle cookies. If you're really lucky, you'll catch their tres leches latte flowing on draft.

901 Berryhill Rd., 704-574-3627
thebatchmaker.com

SOME OTHER SPOTS TO ADD TO YOUR CHARLOTTE SWEET TREAT TOUR

Vicente Bistro
Go for the croissants.
2520 South Blvd., Ste. 108-B, 412-877-7636
vicentebistro.com

Villani's Bakery
Go for a Sfingi.
901 Pecan Ave., 704-334-0550
villanisbakery.com

Manolo's Latin Bakery
Go for a tres leches cake or churros.
4405 Central Ave., Ste. C, 704-568-2120
manolosbakery.com

Jazzy Cheesecakes
Go for the bite-sized cheesecake cupcakes.
1520 Overland Park Ln., Ste. 107
10011 Biddick Ln., Ste. 120, Huntersville, 704-919-1713
jazzycheesecakes.com

Amélie's French Bakery & Café
Go for the macarons or salted caramel brownie.
multiple locations
ameliesfrenchbakery.com

Suárez Bakery
Go for the doughnuts.
4245 Park Rd.
1115 N Brevard St., Ste. 4 (Optimist Hall), 704-525-0145
suarezbakery.com

TASTE YOUR WAY THROUGH CHARLOTTE'S THAI SCENE
STARTING AT BASIL THAI

Some of Charlotte's oldest restaurants are of the Thai variety. For comforting takeout, each neighborhood claims a different favorite, but if you're looking for an upbeat sit-down restaurant (that's also a great double-date spot) Basil Thai in Uptown or Ballantyne is the answer.

Brothers Henry and Chai Eang, who immigrated to the US from Cambodia in the 70s, opened the first Basil Thai in Charleston back in 2002. They brough the popular concept to Charlotte seven years later. The menu has more than a dozen curries, stirfrys, noodles, and rice dishes to choose from. Or you could go with one of their specialities like the red curry duck—a deep-fried boneless half duck, topped with bell peppers, basil, green peas, snow peas, tomatoes, and pineapple.

210 N Church St., 704-332-7212
7800 Rea Rd. A, 704-900-6522
eatatbasil.com

TRY MORE WINNING BITES FROM ANY OF THESE SPOTS

Deejai Thai opened in Myers Park in 2009, and they have a food truck should you ever need an event catered.
613 Providence Rd., 704-333-7884

Thai Taste, one of the more popular options, has been holding it down in Dilworth since 1988.
324 East Blvd., 704-332-0001
thaitastecharlotte.com

Aroy Thai is a bit of an East Charlotte hidden gem.
5301 E Independence Blvd. F, Ste. F, 980-819-5245
aroythaitogo.com

Thai Orchid has been running 30-plus years strong in Strawberry Hill.
4223 Providence Rd., Ste. 7, 704-364-1134
thaiorchidrestaurantcharlotte.com

Thai House is another decades-old restaurant with locations in Pineville, University, Lake Norman, and Cotswold.
thaihouse.us.com

DO BRUNCH
AT EL PURO CUBAN RESTAURANT

El Puro is an authentic Cuban restaurant, owned by Manny Pérez Ochoa; his sister, Ana; and their mother, Dania. The family, which also owns Havana Carolina in Concord, opened El Puro in 2021, in memory of their late patriarch Idael Pérez Maldonado. El Puro has two meanings: an affectionate word for father and a term used in reference to Cuban cigars. From the name to the interior design to each item on the menu, the restaurant is a celebration of Cuban culture, with a fresh twist.

The restaurant is open for lunch and dinner daily (both good options) but on the weekends, this Madison Park hot spot dishes some of the best brunch in Charlotte (and I'm not a brunch person, for the record). If you go, get the tres leches pancakes for the table and try the café bombón—a sweet, creamy espresso-based coffee.

5033 South Blvd., Ste. H, 980-219-8339
elpurocubanrestaurant.com

11

DINE
AT RH ROOFTOP RESTAURANT

Despite being a chain, RH Rooftop Restaurant delivers an experience unlike any other in the city. It's like dining in a luxurious all-season rooftop greenhouse, dripping in chandeliers and greenery with bistro-inspired marble tables, olive trees, cozy seating, and fountains. The menu is as pricey as the luxe decor might suggest, so save this one for a special occasion or when you're in the mood to splash out. My order (Caesar salad, lobster roll, truffle fries, and a glass of bubbly) is north of $80, for instance. The sides are à la carte and plenty large enough to share.

If you go, plan to spend time before or after your meal exploring RH's 50,000-square-foot furniture design gallery for a true main character moment. You can also grab a glass of wine from the bar and stroll the garden patio.

6903 Phillips Place Ct., 704-790-4970
rh.com/us/en/charlotte/restaurant

TIP
If your heart's set on brunch at RH Rooftop Restaurant, a popular option, but you can't grab a seat, put your name on the list at Cafe Monte, a French bakery and bistro also in the Phillip's Place shopping center.

BUILD YOUR OWN CHARCUTERIE BOX
FROM BABE & BUTCHER

Babe & Butcher started building charcuterie boards for private events back in 2019. It sounds cheesy, but these charcuterie boards quickly earned a cult following. So the dynamic duo behind the beloved boards, Lindsay Anvik and Rob Henricks, launched their first brick-and-mortar location two years later in Camp North End.

The build-your-own-box (or board for larger groups) concept is a little like Chipotle: you can pick one or two cheeses, one meat, and up to five complements. These cheeses vary from goat to Gouda, and the complements include snacks like olives, manchego-dusted chips, or dark chocolate. Picnic at Camp North End for a creative first date, bring a box to book club, or stop in for lunch—there's never a bad time for these whimsical, artfully arranged charcuterie boxes.

301 Camp Rd., Ste. 10
4325 Park Rd., Ste. 308, 855-645-5471
babeandbutcher.com

CELEBRATE SOMETHING SPECIAL
AT KINDRED

Kindred's not technically in Charlotte, but it's won many "best restaurant in Charlotte" accolades since it opened in 2015, from local publications to Condé Nast Traveler. The owners, Katy and Joe Kindred, are local food royalty—and not just because Joe's a five-time James Beard Award semifinalist.

The husband-and-wife duo are lauded for their ever-changing, always-inspiring menu and expertly curated wine list. Once you experience Kindred, you'll understand they take their craft seriously, but not too seriously. Their dessert menu features a fat, delightful slice of birthday cake, a playful way to punctuate an elevated meal.

The seasonally driven menu features contemporary twists on Southern cuisine, and you'll always be served their signature salt-topped milk bread to start (it'll be tough, but try not to ruin your appetite for the main course). It's no surprise, I think it should be a rule to order the cake for dessert.

131 N Main St., Davidson, 980-231-5000
kindreddavidson.com

SIP MEZCAL
FROM PUERTA

This upscale Mexican restaurant is one of the buzziest in Charlotte; it's where you go for a fun date night or boozy group dinner. As a 30-something, it's where I go when I want a night out, minus the late-night barhopping. The dimly lit restaurant oozes cool as you enter through the back door and immediately step into their mezcal lounge and bar area where they have a live DJ on weekends. You move through a small passageway into the main dining room, which features a sprawling bar, or out to the front patio that overlooks East 7th Street.

Rightfully so, some of the most popular menu items include the heirloom tomato and Oaxacan cheese salad, queso, empanadas, chipotle short ribs, and any of the tacos. The drink menu features a margarita section and a variety of other mezcal- and tequila-based cocktails, including their take on a (potent) espresso martini.

1961 E 7th St., 704-412-7767
puertaclt.com

TIP

If you don't have a reservation, give them a call and put your name on the waiting list. The wait will likely be long enough for cocktails or apps at the Crunkleton (right next door) or wine at Rosemont (across the street). All three spots are partly owned by legendary North Carolina restaurateur Gary Crunkleton.

DO A NONALCOHOLIC PAIRING
AT RESTAURANT CONSTANCE

Restaurant Constance is easy to cheer for. It's the first from Chef Sam Diminich, who named it after his daughter. The now-chef grew up in the restaurant world and spent years in and out of recovery before returning to his roots. His restaurant is a mile down the road from where he was once homeless using drugs and alcohol—a daily physical reminder of just how far he's come.

Restaurant Constance has a robust wine menu and a full nonalcoholic beverage program—either can be paired with the farm-to-table-style menu. The menu changes, depending on what's available at the local farmers market, but you can expect oysters, short ribs, fish, and pastas. The intimate 10-table restaurant only seats 36 people, and the decor heavily draws on Sam's coastal roots and interests, with shiplap walls, neutral woven chairs, and skateboards and family photos hanging on the walls.

2200 Thrift Rd., 980-549-1999
yourfarmsyourtable.com/reservations

SLURP TRANSFUSIONS
ON SELWYN AVENUE PUB'S PATIO

Selwyn has been the Myers Park neighborhood bar of choice for more than 30 years. The patio is packed year-round, and it has multiple TVs, a bar, firepits, and a mix of lounge and high-top seating. This popular game-day spot has a full menu with typical bar foods like sliders, pizza, chicken tenders, wings, and melts.

    The well-loved watering hole's signature drink is a transfusion, a golf-course classic that suits this golf-loving crowd well. The core ingredients are vodka, ginger ale, grape juice, and lime, but they have multiple takes on the transfusion, including a "skinny" option, a Carolina transfusion made with blue Powerade, and even a seltzer version. No matter which type of transfusion you order, it'll be served in a Selwyn-branded Styrofoam cup with a colored plastic straw.

2801 Selwyn Ave., 704-333-3443
selwynpub.com

17

HAVE A CLASSIC STEAK DINNER
AT BEEF 'N BOTTLE

Charlotte has plenty of flashy steak houses, but if you want a tried-and-true classic, Beef 'n Bottle is your spot. The old-school steak house has been around for more than 60 years, and if walls could talk, I sure would like to know what Beef 'n Bottle's would say. Wood paneling and white tablecloths make this restaurant feel welcoming and worn in (in a good way). With low lighting and low ceilings, even an early-bird dinner feels like an intimate night out here. Like the ambience, the menu is straightforward, and they serve your steak with a giant onion ring on top—no fussy, inedible garnishes here. Salads are served with toppings on the side, so you can craft them to your liking, or you can choose two sides if you want to skip the greens.

4538 South Blvd., 704-523-9977
beefandbottle.net

18

SIP SANGRIA
AT NODA COMPANY STORE

Tiki umbrellas? Check. Porch swings? Check. Tropical landscaping? Check. Quintessential laid-back NoDa vibes? Check. It's easy to see why NoDa Company Store is one of the first places Charlotteans flock to when the weather warms up—or cools down, depending on which side of summer you're on.

Catch up with friends over a famous NoDa Colada, made with fresh coconut and pineapple juices and Prosecco, or introduce your out-of-town family members to the bar's signature sangria. If you prefer something less fruity, there's a selection of beer, wine, and snacks, too.

And you know how people say there's no such thing as a free lunch? Well, that's not true at NoDa Company Store. They've been known to provide free meals for the community on Sundays. You can check their Instagram (@nodacostore) for events and offerings.

3221 Yadkin Ave., 980-859-0441
thecompanystorenoda.com

19

CURE YOUR INDIAN FOOD CRAVING
AT CURRY GATE

Don't let Curry Gate's unassuming exterior fool you. This Nepali and Indian restaurant has some of the most flavor-packed dishes in town. Curry Gate was a success story right out of the gate. It opened in 2020 as a takeout spot and quickly earned a dedicated following as its chaat, kofta, masalas, and curries comforted us through lockdown.

The Dhimal family has continued opening locations across Charlotte to try to meet our insatiable demand. The food speaks for itself, but it's also easy to cheer for the owners, young immigrants dominating Charlotte's food scene. Chuda Dhimal came to Charlotte from Bhutan in 2008, and Nara Dhimal came from Nepal just a few years later. The Dhimal family opened King of Spicy in 2015. This laid-back, popular takeout spot also specializes in Nepalese and Indian dishes.

Curry Gate
5516 South Blvd.
630 W 24th St., 704-712-2968
currygates.com

King of Spicy
5546 Albemarle Rd., 704-900-5475
thekingofspicy.com

OTHER INDIAN RESTAURANTS TO TRY

Botiwalla
From Asheville favorite Chai Pani, Botiwalla is
a casual Indian spot inside Optimist Hall.
1115 N Brevard St., Ste. 203 (Optimist Hall), 980-296-3993
botiwalla.com

Copper
This sit-down Indian spot is located in a historic
Dilworth bungalow and consistently ranks among
Charlotte's best restaurants.
311 East Blvd., 704-333-0063
copperrestaurant.com

Passage to India
A University-area staple, this spot has been
around for more than 15 years.
9510 University City Blvd., Ste. 101, 704-549-1886
passagetoindianc.com

DO A GROUP DINNER (OR LUNCH)
AT CALLE SOL

Calle Sol Latin Café & Cevicheria is in a storied piece of Plaza Midwood real estate that's been home to a number of neighborhood favorites. Restaurateur Frank Scibelli, who also owns Mama Ricotta's, Little Mama's, Yafo, and more, opened Calle Sol in 2021. The casual café has affordable lunch specials by day and is filled with (maybe rum-induced) buzz in the evening.

The menu is inspired by Cuban and Peruvian cuisines, and the interior is as bright and refreshing as the restaurant's signature rum punch. If you go, order salchipapa—Peruvian fries topped with crispy hot dog, a fried egg and ketchup, aji amarillo mayonnaise, and cilantro aioli—for the table. Chaufa is my favorite thing on the menu. It's a simple but flavorful fried rice dish that speaks to the Chinese influence on South American culture that dates back to the 19th century.

>1205 Thomas Ave., 704-565-8291
>3100 Apex Dr., 704-626-1022
>callesolcafe.com

STROLL THROUGH
ROSIE'S COFFEE & WINE GARDEN

A secret garden tucked in an urban setting, this idyllic coffee spot and wine bar is the perfect place to split a bottle for a date or with friends. Picture bistro tables, garden benches, string lights, meandering paths, and verdant archways all throughout the two-acre garden. On chilly nights, they light up the firepits for the coziest, cutest vibe in Charlotte.

They have a small selection of snacks, but you can bring your own food if you want something more robust. For breakfast grab donuts from Reigning Donuts, NoDa's sweetest pick-up window just down the street. For lunch, pick up sandwiches and snacks from Rhino. I go with the cold turkey (turkey, havarti, cucumbers, tomato, lettuce, and dijon on ciabatta), but the chicken torta (pulled chicken, avocado, provolone, jalapeños, lettuce, tomato, and mayo on ciabatta) is an überpopular choice.

940 N Davidson St., 704-604-8975
rosieswinegarden.com

INDULGE IN A DULCE DE LECHE LATTE
AT SUMAQ COFFEE

A gracious patio greets you and airy interiors welcome you in. Soaring ceilings, natural light, and a beautiful tree as the space's centerpiece make the Sumaq Coffee experience well worth it before you even take a bite or sip. The coffee shop is owned by brothers Joseph and Nick Castro, who are originally from Colombia. As such, their menu has a beautiful South American influence with strong drip coffee, empanadas, alfajores, and dulce de leche–flavored desserts and coffee. The organic ambience, paired with delicious drinks and treats, make Sumaq a beautiful, relaxing place to work if you need a change of scenery. Or you can put the laptop away and simply enjoy catching up with a friend or reading that book you never seem to have time for.

6259 South Blvd., 980-585-9437
sumaqcoffeeclt.com

OTHER STOPS FOR YOUR CAFFEINE QUEST

Not Just Coffee
224 E 7th St.
2000 South Blvd.
421 Providence Rd.
2230 Park Rd., Ste.102
1026 Jay St.
notjust.coffee

Stable Hand
125 Remount Rd.
stablehandclt.com

Bitty & Beau's
1930 Camden Rd., Ste. 236
bittyandbeauscoffee.com/location/charlotte

Haraz Coffee House
1204 Central Ave., Ste. 100
harazcoffeehouse.com

Wildroots Coffee
500 E Morehead St., Ste. 106
wildrootscoffee.com

Burr & Berry Coffee
4209 South Blvd.
1221 Transformation Ln., Indian Land
burrandberry.com

Copain Bakery & Provisions
6601 Carnegie Blvd.
copainbakery.com

HOP BETWEEN BREWERIES
IN SOUTH END

Our brewery-centric city has a bevy of options to choose from. So the best way to experience Charlotte's beer scene is to pick a neighborhood and taste your way through a few spots. We have more than 40 breweries across the city, and a strong concentration of them are in South End, making it one of the best spots to plan a hop.

Start with Good Morning Vietnam, a coffee-infused blonde ale from Wooden Robot Brewery. Make your way over to Resident Culture Brewing Company and taste any one of their brews on tap. Refuel at Trolley Barn Fermentory & Food Hall, which has lunch and dinner options aplenty, and you can savor a Sunday Sippin. End your South End brewery crawl at Sycamore where live music might be playing and Mountain Candy IPAs will definitely be flowing.

Wooden Robot Brewery
1440 S Tryon St., Ste. 110
woodenrobotbrewery.com

Resident Culture
Brewing Company
332 W Bland St., Ste. C
residentculturebrewing.com

Sycamore
2151 Hawkins St.
sycamorebrew.com

Trolley Barn
Fermentory & Food Hall
2104 South Blvd.
trolleybarnclt.com

CONTINUE YOUR CHARLOTTE BREWERY TOUR THROUGH ANY OF THESE NEIGHBORHOODS.

PLAZA MIDWOOD
Burial: 1214 Thomas Ave.
Southern Strain: 1800 Central Ave., Ste. A1
Pilot Brewing: 1331 Central Ave., Ste. 104

SOUTHPARK
Legion Brewing: 5610 Carnegie Blvd.
Suffolk Punch: 4400 Sharon Rd., Ste. G23D (behind Dick's Sporting Goods)

NODA/VILLA HEIGHTS
Free Range Brewing: 2320 N Davidson St.
Heist Brewery: 2909 N Davidson St., Ste. 200
NoDa Brewing Company: 2229 N Davidson St.

LOSO
Protagonist Beer: 227 Southside Dr., Ste. A
Gilde Brewery: 3530 Dewitt Ln.
The Olde Mecklenburg Brewery: 4150 Yancey Rd.

GET A TASTE OF THE LOW COUNTRY
AT MERT'S HEART AND SOUL

Mert's Heart & Soul has been dishing up authentic low-country cuisine since 1998. The unpretentious Uptown spot is wildly popular, even President Joe Biden and Guy Fieri—host of *Diners, Drive-Ins and Dives*—have stopped in. Guy called the Soul Roll—a chicken egg roll wrap with collard greens, black-eyed peas and rice—a "soul food missile pop . . . with everything combined in one easy-to-eat bite" on his Food Network show. Luckily, the Soul Sampler includes an order of those famous rolls, along with salmon cakes, cornbread, and fried chicken wings—a solid spread of true Southern fare you can split with the table. If you're shopping for mains, consider the smoked barbecue beef ribs, and do mac and cheese and collard greens on the side for a comforting flavor-packed meal. Saved room for dessert? Mert's has five slices of cake on the menu to choose from—coconut, pound cake, red velvet, strawberry, or chocolate.

214 N College St., 704-342-4222
mertscharlotte.com

25

GRAB
A SANDWICH AND A BEER
FROM THE COMMON MARKET

The Common Market is sort of the antithesis to Charlotte's growing collection of shiny, neutral spaces. I'm not sure there's even an inch of white space; instead, the walls are covered in graffiti, paint, years-old stickers, and flyers. This sandwich shop, market, and neighborhood bar opened 20 years ago in Plaza Midwood and has since expanded to multiple locations.

Pass by any sunny afternoon, and the original location's patio is packed with people drinking craft beers and gathering around the picnic tables. The South End location has a little less grunge and a large, green outdoor space, true to the neighborhood's character. The Oakwold location sits between the Oakhurst and Cotswold neighborhoods.

No matter which location you choose, you can expect casual fare, like bagels, burritos, sandwiches, and bowls. This urban market is also stocked with snacks, bottles of wine, six-packs, and other grocery goods.

235 W Tremont Ave.
2007 Commonwealth Ave.
4420-A Monroe Rd.
commonmarketisgood.com

ORDER LUNCH
FROM PASTA & PROVISIONS

Sure, I could tell you about their amazing homemade pastas or the grab-and-go prepared meals that have saved me more than once when I've volunteered to make dinner. But Pasta & Provisions is often the answer to a very difficult and all-too-common midday mystery: what's for lunch? Yup, this pasta place is a go-to lunch spot with some killer salads and sandwiches.

You could keep it simple with a turkey sandwich, made with smoked turkey, bacon jam, American cheese, avocado, lettuce, tomato, onion, and mayo, all on a toasted hoagie roll. Or you could go big with the Royal Sandwich, stuffed with capicola, sausage patties, provolone, lettuce, tomato, onion, oil, vinegar, and mayo. But if you have room in your schedule for a nap, make it a meatball sandwich.

1528 Providence Rd.
4700 Park Rd.
1600 S Mint St.
pastaprovisions.com

HAVE HAPPY HOUR
AT DILWORTH TASTING ROOM

Work happy hours, date nights, meeting a new friend, celebrating milestones—DTR is appropriate for any occasion worthy of cheers-ing. The original location in Dilworth has lounge seating and a few tables inside, but few things are more delightful than their patio. The expansive, brick outdoor space is surrounded by lush greenery and canopied with string lights. Bistro tables surround the koi pond.

Once a week they do flight nights, which includes a flight of red or white wines and a free personal charcuterie board. It's one of the best deals in the city and a no-fail girls night, in my opinion. For a more robust meal, head to their SouthPark location, which has a larger dining room and an expanded menu so good you'll want to share one of everything.

300 E Tremont Ave.
4905 Ashley Park Ln., Ste. J, 704-595-3337
dilworthtr.com

RECHARGE
AT THE PAULINE TEA-BAR APOTHECARY

The Pauline Tea-Bar Apothecary feels like a warm hug when you walk in. The soothing atmosphere is intentionally created by an herbal aroma, cozy seating options, local art, a wall of mugs, and the friendliest staff you'll ever meet. The lounge and teahouse offers hot and cold tea options—best accompanied by one of their pastries. You get to pick the mug you like most, and the menu tells you the benefits of each tea. Beyond the consumables, Pauline's is designed to be a place of respite and healing. Be warned: you may want to clear your schedule and sink right in once you go. They also host a number of in-person wellness events, like yoga and high tea, vision boarding, and live local music to keep the good vibes going.

2326 Arty Ave.
1017 Beatties Ford Rd., 980-248-2653
thepaulineteabar.com

29

CRUSH A CRAB CAKE
FROM LULU'S

This West Charlotte seafood and chicken restaurant made a name for itself in 2019 when it brought Marylander-approved, baseball-sized crab cakes to the Queen City. Once LuLu's tried to cut costs and remove their signature crab cakes from its menu, but it didn't take long for them to be back, a relief for LuLu's fans far and wide.

What LuLu's takeout restaurant on Tuckaseegee Road lacks in seating and frills, it makes up for with good people and Charlotte's best jumbo lump crab cakes. If the crab cakes don't do it for you (they will), then consider one of their other popular dishes like the chicken and waffles, mac and cheese, or fish and chips—and don't forget a side of crab fries, if you can get your hands on an order.

2400 Tuckaseegee Rd., 704-910-5593

LIGHT UP ALL FIVE SENSES
AT COUNTER-

For years, a criticism of the Queen City was that it lacked "big city" dining options, but in the last half decade or so it's become an exciting place to be a foodie thanks to restaurants like Counter-.

Counter- was founded by James Beard–nominated Executive Chef Sam Hart, and they aim to deliver an ever-evolving range of immersive dining experiences. Everything from the menu to the layout changes to match the theme. Your meal might be paired with visual art, music, and other vehicles to engage all five senses and experience the full food story that Hart and their crew are trying to share. The intimate restaurant typically seats 18 people, and the meal is around 10 to 14 courses. Save this one for a special night out. It's one of the priciest and most unique dining experiences in the city. Don't wait too long—it's only open until September 9, 2032.

2001 W Morehead St., Ste. D, 980-292-2090
counterclt.com

VENTURE INTO VEGAN
AT OH MY SOUL

This South African vegan restaurant is located in a bright blue cottage in NoDa. You order inside that cottage and eat around back, under a giant tent with a 100-year-old oak tree and tons of seating. This vibrant NoDa spot has live music every weekend, too.

The menu is entirely vegan and infused with South African flavor—I promise you won't even miss the meat. Some highlights include the Waka Waka (a spicy lentil patty served with cilantro, tomato, red onion, chilli mayo, guac, chakalaka, and chilli flakes) and a Filthy Fries (French fries with queso, smashed voerie, Pico de Gallo, chakalaka, and peri-peri sauce). On weekends they offer brunch, but luckily you can get a waffle any time. Their cocktails are sneaky good, too. I like the Amagluglug, a South African tequila-based cocktail with guava juice, lime, and mint leaves.

3046 N Davidson St., 704-891-4664
ohmysoulusa.com

GET COZY
AT CUSTOMSHOP

Founded in 2007, Customshop is a Charlotte institution that's earned its way onto many "best" lists. Wood-topped tables, flickering candlelight, a narrow dining room, and a packed bar all set the scene for this unpretentious, high-end spot. The interior is both rustic and retrained, a beautiful foreshadowing of what you'll find on your plate—and in your cocktail glass—at Customshop. The menu changes weekly based on what ingredients are locally available, but it's reliably good thanks to executive chef and owner Andres Kaifer and his crew. The focused menu draws inspiration from Spain, Italy, and France, and it features small plates, pasta, crudo, grilled mains, and a couple of sides. You can order everything to share or save every last bite for yourself.

1601 Elizabeth Ave., 704-333-3396
customshopfood.com

TRUST
THE LANG VAN HYPE

Not many Charlotte restaurants have been around longer or are loved more than Lang Van. In 2020, word got out that the beloved Vietnamese spot was hurting, so restaurant goers started a GoFundMe that raised more than $60,000. Hundreds of holiday cards and thank-you notes hang above the register. The year-round Christmas decor helps to create a cozy, familiar feeling, too.

People love Lang Van for its 100-plus authentic Vietnamese dishes, including pho, noodles, rice, yellow pancakes, and hot pots. But they really love how owner Dan Nguyen never forgets a face and insists on treating everyone like family. If you want a specific recommendation, try a yellow pancake and the bun ga nuong, a well-balanced dish made with mildly sweet chicken, tons of bright fresh veggies, and a little sauce with a slight bite on the side.

3019 Shamrock Dr., 980-443-3160
langvancharlotte.com

34

WATCH AN FC MATCH
AT SALUD CERVECERIA

The James Beard–nominated, Dominican-owned bar has landed a spot on *USA Today*'s "Best Beer Bar" list multiple times. The NoDa nanobrewery is more than just beer, though. It's a place where you can start your day with coffee and pastries and your laptop, have a sandwich served on fresh focaccia and a house-brewed sour in the afternoon, then dance until midnight on weekends.

The neighborhood spot offers something for everyone. Looking for a place to dance? Salud's dance floor comes alive on Latin nights. Kids craving pizza? Salud has wood-fired 'zas with house red sauce (or white). On the hunt for a Charlotte FC game day watch spot? Park it at Salud where you'll be surrounded by like-minded fans—and plenty of food and beer.

3306-C N Davidson St., 980-495-6612
saludcerveceria.com

SAY YES TO YUCA BALLS
AT YUNTA

Maybe it's the Pisco Sour (followed by a Pisco Punch); maybe it's the house music bumping. Either way, this Peruvian-Japanese fusion restaurant is one of the liveliest spots in Charlotte. The interior has an industrial tropical vibe, with a natural-wood-tone accent wall and bar and lush greenery throughout. I've sat at the bar with a friend and gathered around a table with a group, and both times gladly shared multiple dishes. Start with the yuca balls and pick a ceviche to split before diving into something heartier from the grill or wok. The restaurant is small and loud—especially when they have a live DJ—but it's part of the high-energy experience. If you want a more laid-back outing, go on a weekday or a little earlier in the night.

2201 South Blvd., Ste. 130., 980-495-2253
yuntanikkei.com

DO DINNER
AT AL MIKE'S

Charlotte has a glut of trendy restaurants worth adding to your bucket list, but there's a lot of comfort in the classics that helped raise this city. One of those places is Alexander Michael's. It's been around for more than 40 years in an electric-blue Victorian house in the Fourth Ward neighborhood. The building was constructed in 1897 and has long anchored the neighborhood. Before it was a restaurant, it was a general store. Now, it's a true local favorite. (Regulars, don't get too mad at me for writing about it here). It's a casual, publike spot with wood paneling, green walls, and low lighting. You can grab a sandwich to go, sip a beer at the bar, or go for a romantic date night that won't break the bank.

401 W 9th St., 704-332-6789
almikestavern.com

DINE IN A BEAUTIFULLY RESTORED CHURCH
AT SUPPERLAND

Restaurateurs Jeff Tonidandel and Jamie Brown opened Supperland in an old Plaza Midwood church. From the careful architectural preservation to the bespoke custom china, this Southern steak house delivers a special dining experience.

The main dining room greets you with soaring ceilings and exposed brick walls. Booths line the restaurant, and a few counter seats peek into the kitchen. In true Southern fashion, most dishes are meant to be shared. The steaks come sliced, and the miso mac and cheese and other sides are large enough to split.

If you want to experience more Supperland magic, there's a separate stunning, floral-wallpaper-clad bar—the original church sanctuary—with more casual foods like onion dip, brie bites, and oysters. If you fancy yourself a cocktail connoisseur, spring for the spirit experience—a four-course, boozy cocktail pairing in Supperland's speakeasy (shh).

1212 The Plaza, 704-817-7514
supper.land

TASTE EVERY TACO IN TOWN,
STARTING AT NOCHE BRUTA

Tuesday or not, today's a good day for a taco—and thankfully Charlotte has some options for you. A solid introduction to our city's finest tacos is Noche Bruta. Chef Hector Gonzalez-Mora won the city over in 2019 with his breakfast taco pop-ups, and in 2022 he opened El Toro Bruto inside a brewery. He kept his faithful patrons on their toes for a short time, before opening Noche Bruta in spring 2024.

Noche Bruta is inside Hex Coffee, Kitchen & Natural Wines at Camp North End. A few nights a week, you can take your pick from a tight Mexican menu which includes chips and guac, ribeye tacos and churros, among other other items.

201 Camp Rd., Ste.103, 704-899-1696
nochebruta.com

OTHER STOPS ON YOUR TACO NIGHT

Maria's
You're required to order QuesaBirrias—a quesadilla-taco hybrid with cheese and slow-cooked tender beef stew.
5234 South Blvd., 704-525-5075
ordermariasmexican.com

Lupitas Carniceria & Tortilleria
This a family-run butcher shop, has all the ingredients for an authentic at-home taco night.
5316 South Blvd., 980-226-5727
lalupitasnc.com

Tacos el Regio
Find Monterrey-style Trompo Tacos, made from a giant slab of pork cooked on a vertical rotisserie (called a trompo).
8829 E W.T. Harris Blvd., 704-222-9078
tacoselregionc.com

Superica
A go-to spot for trendy Tex-Mex and margs.
101 W Worthington Ave., 980-321-9914
4223 Providence Rd., 704-705-2584
superica.com/charlotte

La Unica
If you've had your taco fill, go for the ACP.
4305 Old Monroe Rd., Indian Trail
900 NC Music Factory Blvd.
16203 Northcross Dr.,Huntersville
4350 Main St., Harrisburg, 704-821-7281
launicarestaurants.com

Tacos El Nevado
One of Charlotte's favorite spots for the classics.
4640 South Blvd., 704-529-4477
4715 Central Ave., 704-563-4667
tacoselnevadonc.com

Camp North End

MUSIC AND ENTERTAINMENT

FIND CREATIVITY AND COMMUNITY
AT CAMP NORTH END

I think it's OK to say this is one the coolest things that's ever happened to Charlotte. Camp North End sits on a 76-acre former industrial site that's now filled with diverse food stalls, public art, and retail shops. It's also a community hub for events, festivals, farmers markets, and more.

With more than 40 unique vendors, this open-air, family-friendly creative hub is a microcosm of Charlotte culture. You can find your next house plant at Grow, or build your collection of records and comics with the help of Hardy Boys, or pick up a used paperback from That's Novel Books. Discover art at Dupp & Swat or Windy O'Connor Art + Home—or just by walking around. Hex Coffee, Kitchen & Natural Wines; La Caseta's Latin American street food; Popbar's frozen treats; and Room Service's craft cocktails are just a few highlights of Camp North End's exciting eateries.

300 Camp Rd.
camp.nc

RIFF THROUGH RECORDS
AT LUNCHBOX

Lunchbox Records has been delighting Charlotte music lovers since 2005. But before it brought its music collection to Charlotte, it started as a punk recording studio and record label in Atlanta in 1990. The brand was dormant for nearly a decade when Scott Wishart decided to dust off the records and bring the Lunchbox magic to our city.

    I don't even own a record player, and the mix of finds at this independently owned record shop still make me giddy. *The Supremes A' Go-Go* sits in the bargain bin for $1; Taylor Swift and Reneé Rapp covers greet mainstream music lovers right up front; and the best of Paramore, Pink Floyd, Pearl Jam, and Panic at the Disco are packed in the "P" section of the record shop. This deeply nostalgic Plaza Midwood shop has thousands of records, along with CDs, old-school tin lunch boxes, and collectibles.

825 Central Ave., 704-331-0788
lunchboxrecords.com

41

LET LIVE MUSIC
MOVE YOU

One of the best parts of living in a growing city is seeing how it answers the question "What do I want to be when I grow up?" And lately, Charlotte's carved its own place in the music industry—making it known we've got more than breweries and banks—with large-scale music festivals.

For years, Breakaway, a traveling music festival, has made a stop in Charlotte on its annual tour. The lineup changes every year, but you can expect two days of music and vibes from a mix of EDM, pop, dance, hip-hop, and house music artists. Past lineups have included popular artists like the Chainsmokers, Martin Garrix, and G-Eazy. In spring of 2024, the inaugural Lovin' Life Music Fest made a splash with headliners like Post Malone, Stevie Nicks, Noah Kahan, DaBaby, Maggie Rogers, and Dashboard Confessional.

breakawayfestival.com
lovinlifemusicfest.com

ENJOY A SHOW
AT THE COMEDY ZONE

If you're looking for a way to shake up your date-night routine, consider a comedy show. The Comedy Zone hosts a number of local and nationally touring stand-up comedians, open-mic nights, and other events. There are shows most Wednesdays through Saturdays, and tickets are reasonably priced.

The venue is cozy, but not so cozy that you're forced to sit close to the stage—a win for people who like stand-up but don't like to be called on. Shows are around 90 minutes to two hours, and its best to arrive early to pick your seat and order food and drinks. The food menu has bar food, like pretzel bites, nachos, wings, and handhelds. If you go, be sure to budget some extra time for parking, especially for the later shows.

900 North Carolina Music Factory Blvd., Ste. B3, 980-321-4702
cltcomedyzone.com

43

CATCH A CONCERT
AT BOFA

Prior to 2019, Bank of America Stadium had only hosted a small handful of concerts in its 20-plus-year-history, including Johnny Cash and June Carter, the Rolling Stones, and Kenny Chesney and Tim McGraw. Opening the venue for business beyond football helped Charlotte land the big-name concerts it had been craving. After all, Bank of America's stadium seats more than three times as many people as the Spectrum Center, an indoor Uptown arena. Since then, we've had several greats roll through town, like Billy Joel, the Rolling Stones (again), the Red Hot Chili Peppers, Elton John, Beyoncé, Luke Combs, Kenny Chesney and Zac Brown Band, and George Strait and Chris Stapleton. The concerts bring more buzz Uptown, too. Toast on Merchant & Trade's rooftop, split oysters at Fin & Fino, or stroll the Monarch Market food hall before the show, then head to Midnight Diner afterward for a late-night bite.

800 S Mint St.
panthers.com/stadium

LOOKING FOR A MORE INTIMATE SHOW? CHECK OUT THESE LOCAL VENUES.

The Underground
820 Hamilton St., 980-266-6460
avidxchangemusicfactory.com/the-underground

The Evening Muse
3227 N Davidson St., 704-376-3737
eveningmuse.com

Visulite Theatre
1615 Elizabeth Ave., 704-358-9200
visulite.com

44

SEE A BROADWAY SHOW
AT BLUMENTHAL

Blumenthal Arts has multiple theaters in Uptown that host a number of shows throughout the year, from annual favorites like *The Nutcracker* to Broadway shows like *Dear Evan Hansen*, *Hamilton*, and *The Lion King*. In addition to Broadway and theater shows, Blumenthal puts on comedy, dance, festivals, and speaking events.

The Blumenthal Performing Arts Center is home to the Belk Theater, Booth Playhouse, and Stage Door Theater. Levine Center for the Arts and Ovens Auditorium are also part of the family. If you really want to commit to a year of performing arts, you can buy season tickets or ticket packages to Opera Carolina, Charlotte Ballet, Charlotte Symphony Orchestra, Tosco Music Party, PNC Broadway Lights Series, or the Equitable Bravo Series.

blumenthalarts.org

TIP

If you want to splash out for a romantic date night, pair your big night out with dinner at La Belle Helene, one of Charlotte's most beautiful restaurants.

300 S Tryon St., Ste. 100, 704-445-4611
labellehelenerestaurant.com

45

TAKE
A SELF-GUIDED MURAL TOUR

Part of the fun is discovering public art by chance, but if you want to organize your own more intentional tour, you can visit the ArtWalks CLT website for itineraries and details about the works, sorted by neighborhood. In South End, you'll find the *Confetti Hearts Wall* by Charlotte artist Evelyn Henson, which just might be one of our city's most-photographed, cheerful spots (West Worthington Avenue). The *Baby Yoda* and *Black Lives Matter* murals by artist Alex DeLarge are NoDa staples. You'll find them right next to each other at NoDa Market & Deli (1721 N Davidson St.). The Uptown Farmers Market's backdrop is a large-scale, can't-miss colorful piece by Curtis King (300 S Davidson St.). And Camp North End alone has more than 30 murals spread across the campus (300 Camp Rd.).

artwalksclt.com

CELEBRATE ART
AT CHARLOTTE SHOUT!

Charlotte's signature arts and culture festival, Charlotte SHOUT!, started in 2019 and celebrates creativity in many forms over two-plus weeks across Uptown. The weeks-long event doesn't take place in one location; there are public art activations and events all over Uptown. In the past, we've had giant seesaws, live mural paintings, larger-than-life blow-up bunnies and gnomes, and pop-up miniature golf courses. Part of the fun is discovering how creatives transform unused spaces, like alleyways, into interactive must-visit destinations. You never know what you'll stumble upon, so lace up some comfy shoes and start exploring with the whole fam. The exact displays and events change each year, but you can expect hundreds of live music events, interactive light installations, games, tasting events, cook demonstrations, and other family-friendly events, typically in April.

charlotteshout.com

ROLL THE DICE
AT LUCK FACTORY GAMES

Codenames? Check. Catan? Check. Clue? Check. With more than 1,000 board games, Luck Factory is where you want to be on a rainy day. The board game café has affordable snack, drink, and beer menus so you can play as many games as you want, for as long as you want.

Done playing? Luck Factory is located in Gibson Mill, a food hall with a number of restaurants/stalls and shops and a brewery. Scour the more-than-750-booth antique mall, the Depot at Gibson Mill. Grab a beer from Cabarrus Brewing Company, Concord and Cabarrus County's first full-scale brewery. Get a homemade scoop from Churn Buddies, or a cookie from Cara's Cookie Company, which supports parents whose infants have a terminal diagnosis. Find burgers and barbecue at Johnny Roger's, or park it at Barcos Sports & Seafood when there's a game on.

305 McGill Ave. NW, Ste. 80, Concord, 704-787-9068
luckfactorygames.com

MAKE A CANDLE
AT PADDYWAX CANDLE BAR

This hands-on candle-making workshop could be your next family outing, team bonding experience, go-to rainy-day activity, or BFF date. Don't worry, no mixologist skills are required. A Paddywax Candle Bar instructor guides you through the scent-mixing and candle-pouring process.

You get to choose from a range of scents and combinations, like violet and vanilla, fresh Meyer lemon, and wild fig and cedar. Take your pick from the dozens of vessels, which are cute enough to be repurposed into drinkware, vases, or storage. You can also order a candle refill kit online.

Candles need a few hours to set, so you can either pick yours up later or have it shipped home for an additional charge. You can book your spot online to guarantee a seat in the 25-to-45-minute workshop.

1930 Camden Rd., Ste. 130, 704-497-6099
thecandlebar.co

49

STROLL THROUGH SOCO

SOCO Gallery is in a 1920s Myers Park bungalow, and it happens to be one of my favorite spots in the city. Art, coffee, coffee table books, and a quiet garden? Don't tempt me with a good time. SOCO (which stands for Southern Comfort) Gallery typically features one or two contemporary artists at a time. Each show opens with artist talks and other in-person programming that gives you an intimate look at the works.

The gallery shares a space with Not Just Coffee and luxury men's clothing store Tabor, so it's best enjoyed if you can linger for a while. Tour the gallery, of course, and let inspiration continue to build as you flip through style, travel, and interior-design books. Treat yourself to a cup of coffee out on the covered porch or in the garden for a soul-nourishing solo date.

421 Providence Rd., 980-498-2881
socogallery.com

50

DANCE THE NIGHT AWAY
AT THE MUSIC YARD

You might not expect one of Charlotte's trendiest late-night music spots to be an open-air pavilion tucked between a barbecue joint and a taco shop, but it is. From electronic DJ sets to house music to rock tribute bands, you can find just about any kind of show at this boutique outdoor music venue. Luckily, if you work up an appetite, SouthBound, the aforementioned attached taco spot, is open until 10 p.m. on weekdays and midnight on weekends. If you prefer the barbecue, Mac's Speed Shop has you covered until 11 p.m. on weekdays and midnight on weekends. Start or end the concert with drinks at BackStage Lounge at SouthBound, a speakeasy just behind the Music Yard. When it's not being used for concerts, the Music Yard also hosts outdoor fitness classes when the weather's nice.

2433 South Blvd., 704-320-6379
musicyardclt.com

FIND YOUR NEW FAVORITE BOOK
AT PARK ROAD BOOKS

In a city full of new, bibliophiles delight in knowing this welcoming independent shop, tucked in a shopping center filled with new, has stayed the same since 1977. You'll always be greeted with the comforting and specific smell of books, and the staff will provide stellar recommendations, if you want them. From local authors to national best sellers spanning every genre, Park Road Books is known for its curated selection and cozy feeling. In the back you'll find kids' book galore and comfy chairs that invite you to stay a while. The shop hosts a number of in-person events, including author talks, book signings, and book clubs. And you just might get to meet Yola, the store dog.

4139 Park Rd., 704-525-9239
parkroadbooks.com

SEE A LIVE SHOW
AT THE NEIGHBORHOOD THEATRE

Another piece of storied real estate, the Neighborhood Theatre has been a part of NoDa's legendary arts scene since 1997. Before that, it was a movie theater for more than two decades. The independent music venue holds a number of concerts throughout the year, but they've also been known to host other live engagements, ranging from an ABBA-inspired disco dance party to a Hillary Clinton campaign event.

Neighborhood Theatre is also home to Yule, Y'all!, Charlotte's annual holiday variety drag show, produced and performed by local queens Robyn O'Ladies and Charlotte Douglas. The 90-minute festive production is filled with original holiday-themed improv, live singing, choreography, and comedy the first weekend of every December. The theater has concessions and a bar slinging cups of holiday cheer for a jolly good time. You can find show details for this year's show via Instagram (@robyncharlotteclt).

511 E 36th St., 704-942-7997
neighborhoodtheatre.com

53

HAVE A SOPHISTICATED NIGHT OUT
AT MIDDLE C JAZZ

Step into Middle C Jazz and soon you'll forget the outside world, as the smooth, energizing sounds fill the intimate Uptown venue. From mainstream to contemporary to R&B and funk, Middle C Jazz brings in a variety of national and local musicians every Wednesday to Sunday night to deliver a show you won't find elsewhere in the city. It's an ideal birthday or anniversary celebration spot, but you don't need a special occasion to delight in this experience.

The jazz club has a robust food menu with tapas to share, like flatbread, crab dip, and calamari. The drink menu has a handful of creatively named craft cocktails, with a creative mix of ingredients, like Wee Baby Blues made with sparkling sangria, cognac, vodka, and peach oleo. There are a bevy of beer and wine options as well.

300 S Brevard St., 704-595-3311
middlecjazz.com

Ice skating in Uptown.
Photo by Andy Weber

SPORTS AND RECREATION

GET YOUR STEPS IN
AT THE RAIL TRAIL

No matter the time of day, this miles-long urban trail is packed with pedestrians, cyclists, electric-scooter riders, and lots of good dogs. The paved path runs from South End to Uptown, right along the Blue Line, so you're never far from a place to grab a bite—or a brew. You can scooter from your Uptown office to Flower Child for a lunch break, or walk to your favorite breweries. In the mood to shop? How about some skin care from Selenite or a 704 shop T-shirt?

   The Rail Trail is also one of Charlotte's most playful public spaces, with rainbow-colored murals, a giant seesaw, an annual pop-up light show, and a number of other interactive elements. Take the family for a nice long walk, followed with a doughnut from the Salty Donut or a Montreal-style bagel from the Good Wurst Co.

charlotterailtrail.org

UNLEASH YOUR INNER ADVENTURER
AT THE US NATIONAL WHITEWATER CENTER

This 1,300-acre adventure park has 50 miles of trails and access to the Catawba River and Long Creek. For the ultra-adventurous, you can try rafting on the man-made whitewater river, or take in the views from a zip line. Looking for more fun? There's rock climbing and ropes courses, too. Non-thrill seekers can hit the trails, people-watch by the rapids, or grab some food or drinks from one of the eateries on-site.

The Whitewater Center has a range of festivals and events throughout the year, including a live music series called River Jam, a winter ice-skating pop-up, and plenty of outdoor yoga classes. Each spring thousands flock to the Whitewater Center for Tuck Fest, their signature celebration of all things outdoors. The three-day festival is jam-packed with live music performances, competitions, clinics, and vendors.

5000 Whitewater Center Pkwy., 704-391-3900
whitewater.org

PLAY PICKLEBALL
AT RALLY

Sure, you could play at a park, but Rally is a pickleballers' paradise with a full (sneaky good) restaurant and bar. Groups of up to 12 people can reserve one of the eight indoor or outdoor courts. Each court comes with its own players' lounge where you can order food and drinks, and your reservation includes paddles and balls. When your playtime runs out, you can watch the action from the sidelines.

You can also join a league or take classes, which are organized by skill level, whether you're brand new to the sport or tournament ready. Looking to make new friends? Consider Cocktails & Courts, a Saturday night league designed for those who are looking to socialize and get a little playing time in. If you want to put your skills to the test, join Rally Ranks—a four-week competitive league.

101 Southside Dr., 980-221-0081
rallypickleball.com

HIKE CROWDERS MOUNTAIN

About an hour drive outside of the city (32 miles west), hiking Crowders is a quintessential Charlotte activity. There are three access points with a variety of trails, ranging from easy to strenuous.

Sparrow Springs has 20 miles of trails, Linwood has four, and Boulders has six. If you're looking for a leisurely hike, park at Sparrow Springs and opt for the Crowders Trail (moderate and 2.8 miles one way) or the Fern or Lake trail loops (easy and under a mile each). Though the Linwood trails are under two miles each way, they're the most difficult.

No matter which adventure you choose, reward yourself with a stop by Veronet Vineyards (1549 Ike Brooks Dr., Kings Mountain) after your hike. You can bring your own food, but the picturesque vineyard also has snacks, including a charcuterie box, and a rotating lineup of food trucks on weekends.

Sparrow Springs access
522 Park Office Ln., Kings Mountain

Linwood access
4611 Linwood Rd., Gastonia

Boulders access
108 Vandyke Rd., Kings Mountain

MAKE NEW FRIENDS (AND GET A LITTLE EXERCISE)
AT MAD MILES RUN CLUB

This Black-led running club, founded by Cornell Jones, attracts hundreds of participants every week. He started running one mile a day in 2019 and spent years building an online community before taking the meetups live. Now, even self-proclaimed nonrunners can't quit this infectious, energized exercise group. Each meetup starts with a live DJ and group stretch. Then you head out for a two-mile run (or walk) that ends in a block party with more dancing and socializing. The club meets Tuesday nights at YVY Training (1701 N Graham St.) and Saturday mornings in Elizabeth Park (101 N Kings Dr.).

The community aspect of the club doesn't stop when you've clocked your miles, though. Mad Miles has given scholarships to student athletes, they've hosted a ball and spades tournament, and most weeks club members keep the party going after the exercise is done.

madmilesrunclub.com

TIP

If you really want to go the distance, sign up for one of Charlotte's signature races, such as the Charlotte Marathon (thecharlottemarathon.com) or the Around the Crown 10K (aroundthecrown10k.com), held each fall.

59

CHEER ON
OUR HOMETOWN TEAMS

Charlotte's steeped in sports history. We've been the home of the Coca-Cola 600 since 1960. In 1993 we landed the Carolina Panthers, after nearly 20 years without an NFL expansion. And it's widely reported people wore tuxedos and gowns for the Hornets debut in 1988.

In more recent history, we scored a major soccer league team, Charlotte FC. Even if you don't fancy yourself a football fan, the energy of the stadium for these matches is electric. Be warned: the supporter section is particularly animated, and it may or may not be tradition to toss your drink when we score.

If your NFL and NBA loyalties lie outside of North Carolina, we've still got plenty of hometown teams to cheer for, including the Charlotte Checkers (AHL) and the Charlotte Knights (MiLB). Both teams have $1 concession specials throughout the season if you're on the hunt for a cheap outing.

TIP
Racing fans should speed over to the NASCAR Hall of Fame in Uptown for a deeper dive into the sport's legacy.
400 E Martin Luther King Jr. Blvd., 704-654-4400
nascarhall.com

60

MAKE A BOUQUET
AT MCLAWLAND FARMS

About a half hour from the city, you can pick flowers and make your own bouquet at McLawland Farms, a 28-acre boutique U-pick farm. Dahlias, sunflowers, zinnias, and cosmos are staples, but owners Jason and Larry are constantly expanding the farm's offerings. Reservations for U-pick flowers and berries are typically open May to October. But you can fully immerse yourself in the urban farm experience any time of year, thanks to their on-site tiny house Airbnb that sleeps up to four guests.

8632 Reedy Creek Rd., 704-804-0937
sites.google.com/view/mclawlandfarms/home

TIP
If you're looking for more farm fun, head to Carrigan Farms where you pick strawberries in spring and summer and sunflowers, apples, and pumpkins each fall. You can also take a dip in the Carrigan Farms quarry when the weather's warm or brave the farm's haunted trails in October.
1261 Oakridge Farm Hwy., Mooresville, 704-664-1450
carriganfarms.com

HEAD TO MOOD HOUSE
FOR THE ULTIMATE SELF-CARE SOLO DATE

If you're craving self-care, carve out an hour or so at Mood House. The modern massage studio, founded by Cristina Wilson, offers 50- and 80-minute massages, infrared sauna sessions, and a meditation room. For the ultimate wellness mini retreat, book a sauna session right after your massage.

For your massage, you can pick one of four moods to guide your session. Is your to-do list running your life? Calm will send you into a slow, deep relaxation. Going through a work slump? Clear will inspire the focus and creativity you need. Trying to practice more gratitude? Abundant should do the trick. Looking for more pep in your step? Awake could foster those energetic vibes. Each mood is paired with an aromatherapy blend and breathwork for a true "mind, body, mood" experience.

2400 Park Rd., Ste. A, Dilworth
4008 Monroe Rd., Oakhurst Commons, 704-286-0906
thisismoodhouse.com

TIP

Head to Green Brothers Juice and Smoothie Co. for a smoothie afterward. I like to bring a journal so I can jot down anything that may have come up during my massage.

62

PEOPLE-WATCH
AT THE WELLS FARGO CHAMPIONSHIP

One of the city's prized annual events, the Wells Fargo Championship—which will be under a new name in 2025—draws thousands to Quail Hollow Club every spring to catch their golf heroes in action. From Tiger Woods to Rory McIlroy, the tournament's hosted many greats. But it's just as much a social event with some of the best people-watching the Queen City has to offer. Many people wear casual, sporty clothing, but, in very Southern fashion, you'll also see groups dressed in their garden-party-like best.

For food and drink options, the Wells Fargo Championship typically has stands scattered throughout the course with things like beer, lemonade, and pretzels, and a marketplace with local vendors and expanded options. If you're willing to shell out for top-tier tickets, you get access to private drink-inclusive clubs with private bathrooms, covered seats, and concessions.

3700 Gleneagles Rd.
wellsfargochampionship.com

TIP
Wear sunscreen and comfortable shoes. You can expect limited shade and miles of walking around the course. And if you can make it on a weekday, practice rounds are typically cheaper and less crowded.

GLIDE INTO THE HOLIDAY SPIRIT WITH ICE-SKATING
AT THE WHITEWATER CENTER

Outdoor ice rinks pop up every holiday season around Charlotte, bringing us as close to a white Christmas as our mild weather allows for. The Whitewater Center has multiple ice trails and free-skate areas, plus an on-ice Airstream that has hot and cold drinks for sale when you need some fuel.

Outdoor rinks are open mid-November through mid-February, roughly. But if they're too crowded for your liking, or you have the urge to ice-skate off-season, try an indoor rink like Extreme Ice Center in Indian Trail or Pineville Ice House.

The Whitewater Center
5000 Whitewater Center Pkwy., 704-391-3900
whitewater.org

MORE ICE SKATING FUN

Truist Field
Skate surrounded by skyline views
and a European-inspired market.
324 S Mint St., 704-274-8282
milb.com/charlotte-knights

Camp North End
400 Camp Rd., 980-337-4600
camp.nc

Carowinds' WinterFest
14523 Carowinds Blvd., 704-588-2600
carowinds.com/events/winterfest

Extreme Ice Center
This is an indoor rink for all seasons.
4705 Indian Trail Fairview Rd., Indian Trail, 704-882-1830
xicenter.com

Pineville Ice House
Another great indoor rink for all seasons.
400 Towne Centre Blvd., Pineville, 704-889-9000
pinevilleice.com

GET YOUR ADRENALINE PUMPING
AT CAROWINDS

Carowinds was made for thrill seekers. The amusement park has more than 60 rides, from kid-friendly coasters to terrifying drop towers. Fun fact: the park sits on the North and South Carolina border, so you'll visit two states in one day.

In the summer, you can cool off in the 26-acre waterpark, which has waterslides, wave pools, private cabanas, and kiddie areas. The theme park also has a number of seasonal signature events. On fall nights, Carowinds transforms into a spooky theme park called SCarowinds with haunted houses and mazes, scare zones, and horror shows. Shortly after, holiday magic takes over and festoons the park in shimmering lights and festive displays for WinterFest. Expect ice-skating, live holiday-themed performances, and visits with Santa.

14523 Carowinds Blvd., 704-588-2600
carowinds.com

HIKE
ALONG A GREENWAY

No matter where you are in North Carolina, you can access nature within minutes—and Charlotte is especially green. Mecklenburg County has more than 70 miles of greenway trails that run throughout our communities, and one day, if all goes according to the county's plan, we'll have 300-plus miles. Many of the greenways connect parks, neighborhoods, and shopping centers.

If you want to explore Birkdale Village, walk the 1.5-mile McDowell Creek Greenway, which runs through the Huntersville shopping center. You're going to want to fuel up with a burger from Bad Daddy's. Or maybe you want to make getting to Freedom Park an adventure of its own. In that case, hop on Little Sugar Creek Greenway. Try Four Mile Creek Greenway for a paved and boardwalk-covered trail, surrounded by natural landscape—which comes in clutch during sweltering Charlotte summers.

Visit parkandrec.mecknc.gov for additional trailheads and more details.

TAKE AN EPIC WEEKEND GETAWAY
TO CHARLESTON

One of Charlotte's calling cards is its central location. We're driving distance from the beach and mountains. Charming cobblestone streets, multiple beaches nearby, and some of the best dining in the Southeast make Charleston a worthy first stop on your Carolina road-trip series.

Caffeinate and get a pastry or slice of quiche from Harken before meandering through downtown, admiring the rainbow-colored architecture and shopping along King Street. If you're an art lover, or want a respite from the heat, stop by the Gibbes Museum of Art. Check into your hotel; the Palmetto or Zero George will do just fine. Do a rooftop happy hour at the Citrus Club, followed by dinner at Vern's or Leon's Fine Poultry & Oyster Shop. Day two, pick up sandwiches from The Pass, and spend the day basking in the sun on Sullivan's Island, with some frosé from the Co-Op to keep you cool.

Harken
62 Queen St., 843-718-3626
harkencafe.com

Gibbes Museum of Art
135 Meeting St., 843-722-2706
gibbesmuseum.org

The Palmetto Hotel
194 E Bay St., 843-823-3604
palmettohotelcharleston.com

Zero George
0 George St., 843-817-7900
zerogeorge.com

Citrus Club
334 Meeting St., 843-872-9063
thedewberrycharleston.com/citrus-club-policies

Vern's
41 Bogard St. A
vernschs.com

Leon's Fine Poultry & Oyster Shop
698 King St., 843-531-6500
leonsoystershop.com

The Pass
207-A St Philip St., 854-444-3960
thepasschs.com

Co-Op
2019 Middle St. (Sullivan's Island), 843-882-8088
thecoopsi.com

67

PUT THOSE IMAGINARY GOLF SWINGS TO GOOD USE
AT PUTTERY

It's no surprise that Charlotte, a golf-loving community, has a number of Putt-Putt and golf-lite options, from no-frills driving ranges to fancy private clubs with virtual courses. If you're a drinking-age group looking for an activity—rain or shine—Puttery has two themed indoor mini golf courses and a full bar menu. The concept may be backed by professional golfer Rory McIlroy, but no experience is required. You can eat/drink while you play, or you can order from and hang in the lounge.

210 Rampart St., 704-368-1600
puttery.com/locations/charlotte

TIP

Have a little more golf experience? Hit up Leatherman's for date night. You can practice your drives with a bucket of balls and beer for around $30. They also offer private lessons if you want to get serious about your game.

PADDLE
ON THE CATAWBA

For an easygoing, quick paddle, consider the Lake Wylie Dam to Riverwalk trail. This 3.5-mile excursion starts at the Lake Wylie Dam Access Point (2541 New Gray Rock Rd., Fort Mill) and ends at Riverwalk Rock Hill (575 Herrons Ferry Rd., Rock Hill), which has restaurants and more adventures to be had at the Rock Hill Outdoor Center at Riverwalk.

Looking for a longer paddle? Park at Catawba Nation Hand Carry Boat Launch (1175 Charley Horse Rd., Rock Hill) and finish at Landsford Canal State Park (2051 Park Dr., Catawba) for an easy, 9.7-mile trail.

The Catawba River has multiple free access points, but if you need a one-stop shop, consider the Whitewater Center. You can rent single or tandem kayaks, or stand-up paddle boards, and they provide a life vest.

EXPLORE
SEVEN OAKS NATURE PRESERVE

Easier than a mountain hike, more strenuous than a sidewalk stroll, the Seven Oaks Nature Preserve trail is an idyllic way to spend time outdoors. The scenic path wraps around a portion of Lake Wylie and runs through Daniel Stowe Botanical Garden. The entire loop trail is around five miles total. The trail is open year-round, but be mindful of rain. Some sections are incredibly muddy, so I avoid this trail the day after a rainstorm.

Pack a picnic and make a pit stop at Daniel Stowe Botanical Garden; it's well worth the admission fee to stroll the impressive grounds and exhibits. If you don't want to carry a cooler, you can buy snacks, wine, and drinks at the Garden Store on-site. The gardens are gorgeous in spring, but the trail is especially magical when the leaves start changing in fall.

Parking/trailhead
6900 S New Hope Rd., Belmont

Daniel Stowe Botanical Garden
6500 S New Hope Rd., Belmont, 704-825-4490
dsbg.org

70

PICK YOUR PRODUCE
FROM A FARMERS MARKET

Lucky for those who call Charlotte home, we have multiple major markets that offer the riches of the Piedmont region. The Matthews Community Farmers' Market is as local as it gets with a number of Charlotte small food businesses and high-quality, locally grown produce including Micro greens, regular-sized greens, jams, herbs and fresh flowers.

Find fresh fish caught off the North Carolina coast at Charlotte Fish Co. Get your barbecue fix from Ernie's Smokehouse. Order the best breads from Verdant or Team Rose Bread. Reap Urban Gourmet Farms' mushroom harvest.

188 N Trade St., Matthews
matthewsfarmersmarket.com

TIP
Start your morning with a coffee from Brakeman's Coffee & Supply and do a little shopping at Moxie Mercantile before strolling through the market. All stops are within walking distance.

KEEP PERUSING FOR PRODUCE.

The Charlotte Regional Farmers Market
A wide selection, from microgreens to bouquets to meats, that sprawls across multiple warehouses in high season.
1801 Yorkmont Rd.

Uptown Farmers Market
An urban market, with one of the best mural backdrops in town.
300 S Davidson St.

South End Farmers Market
Bustling with a mix of local artisans, crafts, and produce stands.
2000 South Blvd.

Kings Drive Farmers Market
A Charlotte favorite with a strong selection of seasonal produce, plus it transforms into a pumpkin patch in the fall and a Christmas tree lot in the winter.
939 S Kings Dr.

Bechtler Museum of Modern Art

CULTURE AND HISTORY

PLACE YOUR ANNUAL BAKLAVA SUNDAE ORDER
AT THE GREEK FEST

One of Charlotte's oldest and largest cultural events, the Yiasou Greek Festival draws tens of thousands of visitors each fall. There are live performances and artisans and carnival rides and games for the kiddos, but the main attraction is the food. Cars and people line the Dilworth neighborhood to get their annual Greek festival fix. On the savory side, grab a gyro, sandwiches, fries, spanakopita, and other Greek dishes. The festival has a few famous sweets, including the greek honey doughnuts, frappes, and their signature baklava sundaes (ice cream topped with baklava). You might want to go with a group so you taste a little bit of it all. Or if you're on the go, they've got you covered with the drive-thru. It's set up at the corner of East Worthington and Winthrop Avenues, and you can order combination dinner plates, pita sandwiches, and assorted pastry boxes.

600 East Blvd., 704-334-4771
yiasoufestival.org

BUY LOCAL ART
AT BLKMRKTCLT

BlkMrktClt, co-owned by artist Dammit Wesley and Sir Will, hosts the Hunnid Dollar Art Fair—an annual pop-up art sale—each holiday season during Camp North End's Mistletoe Market. The sale started as a way to help artists clear out their inventory and has grown into a larger seasonal affair that platforms dozens of talented people from around the region. The Hunnid Dollar Art Fair is also meant to make professional artwork more accessible, especially for those just starting to build their collections. If you go, you can expect original works and prints, right around $100, as well as a selection of full-priced works. The sale typically happens in December, but you can support Black artists all year long at BlkMrktClt, a contemporary studio and gallery space for photographers and artists. Make an appointment to tour.

blkmrktclt.com

PLAY ART CRITIC
AT THE MINT

North Carolina's first art museum, The Mint has been around since 1936 and has expanded to two locations. The Uptown location—right next to the Bechtler Museum of Modern Art—features American art, contemporary art, and design as part of its permanent collection. If you head to the Eastover location, you'll find a European and African art, ancient art, and ceramics. Both locations regularly host exciting exhibitions that celebrate everything from furniture craftsmanship to Picasso Landscapes to contemporary Southern art.

Beyond exhibits, The Mint has a jam-packed social calendar with regular artists talks and community yoga classes, along with annual events like Art In The Garden tours. Young Affiliates of The Mint, one of Charlotte's most popular young professional groups, hosts the decades-long Derby Days tradition, filled with Mint Juleps, fascinators, and Kentucky Derby viewing.

500 S Tryon St.
2730 Randolph Rd., 704-337-2000
mintmuseum.org

TIP
Both locations are free on Wednesday evenings.

74

TAKE THE KIDDOS
TO THE GREAT ELIZABETH PUMPKIN WALL

Charlotte often feels like a big little city, and community traditions like the annual Great Elizabeth Pumpkin Wall lighting make it so. For the last two decades, the Elizabeth neighborhood has filled a 60-foot-long wall with dozens of jack-o'-lanterns, carved by its community members.

About a week before Halloween, the jack-o'-lanterns are lined up and put on display for the grand reveal, during which the word of the year is shared in a New Year's Eve countdown-like ceremony. The words started as overtly political yard messages but have since become a broader reflection of culture and the spirit of the historic neighborhood. The word, illuminated and outlined by lights, has been things like "vote" in 2018, "together" in 2020, and "harmony" in 2022.

Hundreds of Charlotteans gather from around the city to see the spectacle and theme of the year.

The exact location and dates are shared on elizabethcommunity.com.

75

CELEBRATE BLACK CULTURE AND COFFEE
AT ARCHIVE CLT

A coffee shop that's more than a coffee shop, Archive is a celebration of Black culture. Photos of Black icons hang on the walls, and there are shelves full of books, art, records, and other ephemera for sale. As a magazine girl myself, I especially love the stacks of vintage magazines and editorial pages pasted to the bathroom walls. The storied shop also hosts in-person events like poetry readings, yoga, book signings, movie nights, photography showings, and other events celebrating Black works.

You can grab your coffee to go, or sit down and stay a while to soak in the inspiration. The coffee menu features coffees, hot teas, iced tea refreshers, and flavored drinks like the "Foxy Brown Latte" which is made with a sweet and savory brown butter sauce.

2023 Beatties Ford Rd., Ste. D, 980-800-5575
archiveclt.com

TASTE BITES
BY BLACK CHEFS

Since 2017, Black Food Truck Friday has made answering "what's for dinner" a whole lot easier—at least one day a week. The lineup and location rotates, but most Fridays you can expect a solid lineup of Black-run food trucks to choose from, plus other vendors and food and drink options. Follow @blackfoodtruckfridays on Instagram for schedule updates.

Continue celebrating Black chefs at the annual BayHaven Food & Wine Festival. In 2021, Charlotte restaurateurs Greg and Subrina Colliers started the festival as a way to uplift Black chefs and mixologists, celebrate excellence, and share history and stories through food. The festival is typically days long, starting with a series of intimate multicourse, sit-down meals you can take part in. A tasting ticket gets you access to more than 50 renowned Black food and drink vendors from across the US, so it's your best opportunity to taste as much as possible. Foodies who don't mind spending the extra dough can opt for one of the dinners to go even deeper.

bayhavenfoodandwine.com

GET YOUR TURKEY LEG FIX
AT CAROLINA RENAISSANCE FESTIVAL

Jousting on horseback, giant turkey legs, falconry shows, archery competitions, ale and mead—the Carolina Renaissance Festival has it all. Thousands of peasants, dragons, knights, kings, queens, and fairies flock to Fairhaven each fall to indulge in the old-time fun. You can shop arts and crafts from more than 100 vendors at the village's open-air artisan market. Kids can climb a tower, hop on carnival rides, ride a camel, pet some animals, and participate in a number of other activities and games. Jousting takes place three times a day, 500 costumed characters help bring the Renaissance to life, and there are 16 stages of entertainment with nonstop shows. You'll certainly leave stuffed if you dine your way through the fair's share of eateries, hocking skewered meats, stews, bread bowls, pastries, and brews.

carolina.renfestinfo.com

78

DISCOVER SOMETHING NEW
WITH THE FAMILY

A rainy-day savior, Discovery Place has a number of interactive kids museums throughout Charlotte, including Discovery Place Science in Uptown and Discovery Place Kids in Huntersville and Rockingham. Let the little ones unleash their inner explorer and tap into imaginative play at Discovery Place Kids. Families can experiment in labs or experience Earth's biodiversity with a range of hands-on exhibits and catch an IMAX movie at Discovery Place Science. Once a month, the museum is closed to the kiddos for Science on the Rocks; adults get to experience childlike fun, with a cocktail in hand, at this after-hours event.

Construction started on a newly imagined Discovery Place Nature in 2024, with big plans for a free garden with native plants, wildlife, an otter exhibit, learning labs, and a canopy skywalk.

Discovery Place
704-286-8302
discoveryplace.org

Discovery Place Science
301 N Tryon St.

Discovery Place Nature
1658 Sterling Rd.

Dicscovery Place Kids
105 Gilead Rd., Huntersville
233 E Washington St., Rockingham

TIP
Discovery Place also runs fun, science-infused summer camps for kids in Kindergarten to 6th grade.

GET INTO THE HOLIDAY SPIRIT
AT THE SOUTHERN CHRISTMAS SHOW

Every November, my aunt and I go to the Southern Christmas Show for top-tier people-watching, and to get an early, hefty dose of Christmas spirit. People travel from all over the region, and you'll often see groups in matching holiday-themed T-shirts with the year printed on them. The hardcore shoppers bring wagons and fill them with seasonal decor and gifts. Less ambitious shoppers like me spring for a commemorative reusable tote for their goods.

You can expect hundreds of vendors selling things you never knew existed, like gourds painted as the Grinch or coasters for your car's cupholders. The show has dozens of decorated trees, visits with Santa, and holiday performances. It's typically held the third week of November at Bojangles Coliseum.

800 Briar Creek Rd. (The Park Expo and Conference Center)
southernchristmasshow.com

LET THE LIGHTS DAZZLE YOU
AT CHRISTMAS TOWN U.S.A.

A little town outside of Charlotte called McAdenville transforms into Christmas Town U.S.A. each December with a Hallmark-holiday-movie-worthy light show. Like most homegrown traditions, it started with a few neighbors who wanted to decorate the community trees in classic red, green, and white Christmas lights. The holiday cheer was infectious, and now, more than 60 years later, half a million lights adorn 100 or so homes, illuminated Christmas trees float on the community lake, and 250 evergreens are decked in dazzling lights. Though you're welcome to drive through, people are encouraged to experience the enchantment on foot. Take a lap around the 1.3-mile lake for maximum yuletide joy. The tree lighting ceremony is typically held December 1, and the lights are on nightly from 5:30 to 10 p.m. through December 26.

212 Wesleyan Dr., McAdenville
townofmcadenville.org/visitors/christmas-town-usa

CELEBRATE PRIDE MONTH...
IN AUGUST

June is National Pride Month, but Charlotte Pride celebrations are held in August, including our annual Pride Parade. Uptown buildings are lit in rainbow colors, flags wave through the streets, and more than 200,000 LGBTQIA+ community members and allies attend the annual celebrations.

Though the Charlotte Pride organization wasn't formally founded until 2000, Pride celebrations started gaining traction in Charlotte in the 1980s. In 1994, we hosted the NC Pride March. An estimated 4,000 people attended, the most the state had seen since the inaugural march. In 2001, the Charlotte Pride Festival took over Uptown's Marshall Park, and finally the parade came in 2013.

Charlotte Pride hosts other events throughout the year, including Charlotte Pride Festival and Parade; Charlotte Latinx Pride; Charlotte Trans Pride; Charlotte Women's Pride; Charlotte Pride Interfaith Programs; and Reel Out Charlotte, an annual LGBTQIA+ film festival.

charlottepride.org

82

TAKE A CULINARY ROAD TRIP
TO JON G'S

I wouldn't be a very good North Carolina tour guide if I didn't give you a barbecue recommendation. So, I suggest you make it a road trip and head about an hour east to Jon G's. *Southern Living*, *Eater*, *Thrillist*, and even *Texas Monthly* have put their stamp of approval on this roadside Texas barbecue joint. It's only available on Saturdays, and people start queuing up for their 'cue around 9am (it opens at 11am). Pulled pork, Cheerwine sausage, brisket, jalapeno cheese grits, brown sugar smoked beans and other Southern delicacies are dished out until they're gone. If you want to add a little Eastern Carolina flavor to your plate, you can add Jon G's sweet vinegar sauce—but Texans will say you don't need it.

To round out your Southern culinary road trip, you can drive about 10 minutes down the highway for fresh peach ice cream (and plain old peaches, if you want) from Peaches n' Cream at 2735 US 74 in Wadesboro. If you see a giant peach ice cream cone cutout on the side of the road you're in the right place.

Jon G's Barbecue
116 Glenn Falls St., Peachland
704-272-6301
jongsbarbecue.com

EXPERIENCE AFTERNOON TEA
AT CHEZ MARIE PÂTISSERIE

Herringbone wood floors, an archway of flowers, and the prettiest pastry case set the scene for this upscale French café. You can stop in for coffee, tea, or treats any time, but if you want the royal experience, make a reservation for afternoon tea—France's answer to the British high tea tradition.

Afternoon tea is $25 and includes a personal teapot and a triple tower of treats, including savory sandwiches and a sampling of sweets like macarons, éclairs, or madeleines. You get to pick your tea, but towers are the chef's choice. Let them know ahead of time if you have any allergies or restrictions.

Looking for more? The Ballantyne Hotel also does high tea on weekends. It's twice the price for adults, but you get more food and have the option to add bubbles.

4732 Sharon Rd., Ste. M, 704-910-3013
chezmarieclt.com

SOAK IN CHARLOTTE HISTORY
IN UPTOWN

For 50 years, the Harvey B. Gantt Center for African-American Arts + Culture has been celebrating Black history and culture. The storied museum is named appropriately after our first Black mayor and Clemson's first Black student Harvey B. Gantt. Stroll through the galleries to see a rotating lineup of exhibitions, or grab a ticket to one of their events. The museum regularly hosts a number of special events, including live music, food events, talks with Black thought leaders and more.

After you've soaked in all you can, take a three-minute walk over to the Levine Museum of the New South where you can learn more about Charlotte's history and what it means in the context of today. Want to go deeper? The museum has a number of family friendly cultural celebrations, author talks and other opportunities to engage in conversations about culture and history.

Harvey B. Gantt Center for African-American Arts + Culture
551 S Tryon St., 704-547-3700
ganttcenter.org

Levine Museum of the New South
401 S Tryon St., 704-333-1887
museumofthenewsouth.org

COOK UP SOME FUN
WITH CHEF ALYSSA

Chef Alyssa has been turning Charlotteans into home chefs with her cooking classes since 2013. You can learn foundational French cooking techniques or enroll in a basic meal boot camp at Chef Alyssa's Kitchen. The classes are tailored to skill level, whether you've never picked up a knife or are hungry for a culinary challenge.

Potato and Manchego croquettes with piquillo pepper aioli, paella with chicken and shaved chorizo, grilled lamb with rosemary and hot paprika-honey drizzle, and chocolate cake with hazelnut ice cream—those were all on the menu for an intermediate Spanish tapas class. Going gluten free? How about learning to make sorghum-glazed baby carrots, seared snapper with spring garlic and aleppo chili butter, and polenta with caramelized spring onions? The exact offerings change, but you can expect most classes will include three or four dishes and last three hours.

4001-C Yancey Rd., Ste. 100, 704-817-7568
chefalyssaskitchen.com

FIND NONALC COMMUNITY
WITH COUNTERCULTURE CLUB

We've established that Charlotte loves a brewery, but there's also a noticeable effort among establishments to offer more nonalcoholic drink options, and a noticeable craving for experiences where alcohol is decentered—or not present at all. That's where the Counterculture Club comes in. Molly Ruggere, who founded the popular club, hosts a variety of social events that don't involve alcohol including yoga, holiday gatherings, book clubs, and panels around topics like dating and sobriety throughout the year.

She also started Charlotte's first nonalcoholic Counterculture Festival. It has a lot of the hallmarks of a beer festival—tastings, for-sale beverages, and live music and entertainment—but without the alcohol. Instead, you can taste samples from national and local nonalcoholic brands. Past events have included tarot readings and a live podcast recording. The festival takes place in January, a time when many are looking for hangouts, hold the hangover.

countercultureclub.org

EDIT Sale

SHOPPING AND FASHION

87

PERUSE THE PROVISIONS
AT REID'S FINE FOODS

This nearly century-old gourmet grocery store is one of Charlotte's oldest restaurants. Since its Morehead Street debut, Reid's has changed hands, relocated, and expanded throughout the city. With its signature green-and-white interiors, marble counters, bistro tables, and fancy snacks, it's the poshest place to grocery shop. Order a sandwich from the counter, or wine from the bar, then stroll through the aisles of specialty snacks and regional produce.

The SouthPark location has a sit-down restaurant with an expansive covered patio and robust menu. When the weather's nice, nothing beats a glass of rosé, salad, and truffle fries on the Reid's patio, especially when they have live music. Looking for a deal? Grab half-priced steak burgers on Tuesdays. No matter which location you go to, be sure to bring home a slice of cake. Reid's layered cake is one of my favorite desserts in the city.

2823 Selwyn Ave.
4331 Barclay Downs Dr.
121 W Trade St., Ste. 150
135 Levine Ave. of the Arts, Ste. 120
reids.com

HUNT FOR HOME DECOR
AT HOUSE OF NOMAD

House of Nomad is a full-service design studio created by North Carolina natives Berkeley Minkhorst and Kelley Lentini. The duo is known for their globally inspired aesthetic that brings the essence of travel home. The designers opened a SouthPark storefront, making their same cultured and curated aesthetic more accessible for those not in the market for a home makeover.

The House of Nomad store touches on all areas of home from beautiful glass decanters in shades of smoke and amber to rainbow-colored Turkish rug runners. Give your living room a more sophisticated look with a pair of acrylic and brass table lamps, and buy the host in your life a thoughtful coffee table book and some wavy wineglasses—all in one fell swoop, thanks to this stylish home decor shop.

4401 Barclay Downs Dr., Ste. 132, 980-585-1007
houseofnomaddesign.com

89

SCORE SECONDHAND DESIGNER FASHIONS
AT THE EDIT SALE

Twice a year, Charlotte's most stylish women scout an open warehouse and fill it with thousands of pieces of deeply discounted, gently used (and often new with tags) designer clothing and accessories. The sale started as a clothing swap between Stephanie Bissell, Shelly Landau, and Jennifer Shelton in Jennifer's garage in 2016. As word got out, more of their friends wanted in, and the fashion-loving trio launched the EDIT Sale. The sale is all about a communal in-person shopping experience and sustainable, intentional shopping practices.

The pop-up sale is held each spring and fall, and savvy shoppers line the block on opening day to get in. You can find brands like Gucci, Chanel, Ganni, Ulla Johnson, La DoubleJ, Sue Sartar, Erdem, Rosie Assoulin, and Dries Van Noten for up to 90 percent off retail—a steep discount, but still not bargain-bin pricing.

editsale.com

TIP

If you do go on day one, the line could be hours long. The dressing room is shared, so wear undergarments you're comfortable in.

FIND SOMETHING FUNKY
AT THRIFT PONY

Colorful cowboy boots, a vintage Coach bag, a high-quality trench coat, and a crop top that says "young ex-wife"—those are all things you might find at Thrift Pony. The Plaza Midwood consignment shop is the brainchild of fashion entrepreneur Hellen Moffitt. It started as a clothing delivery service (like a local Rent the Runway) and expanded into a brick-and-mortar thrift shop.

While the delivery service is no longer, Hellen has leaned into her shop and überpopular pop-up thrift markets. You'll find well-priced apparel and accessories from places like Anthropologie, Free People, Zara, and Abercrombie—along with one-of-a-kind vintage pieces—typically priced from $5 to $50. She's recently taken her show on the road, so you might see her mini pink school bus wheeling through town or parked at local events.

1110 Morningside Dr., Ste. E, 803-526-7264
thriftpony.com

STILL HUNTING FOR A THRILLING FIND? CHECK OUT THESE OTHER SECONDHAND SHOPS.

The Rat's Nest
Ultra-cool shop with a 1970s and Western flair.
442 E 36th St., 704-371-3599

Stash Pad
Curated collection of retro pieces.
2708 Monroe Rd., 980-237-8381
stashpadvintage.com

Street Commerce
Luxury street-style shop.
325 E 9th St., 704-891-8833
streetcommerce.shop

JT Posh
High-end luxury consignment.
2400 Park Rd., Ste. 2A, 704-375-1334
jtposh.com

SHOP 'TIL YOU DROP
AT PHILLIPS PLACE

Phillips Place has long been one of Charlotte's luxury shopping destinations. And it's recently gone through a major overhaul, welcoming new-to-Charlotte retailers like Jenni Kayne, Ralph Lauren, alice + olivia, and Veronica Beard. Grab a coffee from Ralph's signature green coffee truck and window shop until you drop.

Find the sequin caftan with feather trim you never knew you needed at Dallas-based La Vie Style House. Or say yes to the dress at Ladies of Lineage, if you're in the market for a designer wedding gown. Or shop elevated menswear at Taylor Richards & Conger, which has been making Charlotte men more stylish for more than 30 years.

6800 Phillips Place Ct.
phillipsplacecharlotte.com

TIP

If you need a little sustenance, grab a bite from 800 Degrees, which serves pizza, salads, and sandwiches all day long—plus hearty entrées for dinner.

6815 Phillips Place Ct., 980-880-4800
800degreescarolinas.com

GET LOST
IN SLEEPY POET

A treasure hunter's paradise, Sleepy Poet Antique Mall is a 48,000-square-foot warehouse with an eclectic mix of finds, including vintage vinyl records, quirky pieces of clothing from the 1930s through the 1980s, cowboy boots, retro home accessories, wacky wall hangings, and antique furniture. The price points and offerings vary widely, so don't be afraid to take a few laps around the mall before deciding what to bring home.

Still on the hunt for the perfect piece for your pad? Find a treasure trove of traditional home decor and furniture at Classic Attic in Park Road Shopping Center. Shop more than 70 vendors and artists in one spot at Cotswold Marketplace. Rummage through rugs and fabulous furniture from South End Exchange. Or score something totally one-of-a-kind at Slate Interiors.

6424 South Blvd., 704-529-6369
sleepypoetstuff.com

93

FIND CURVY COUTURE
AT JUICY BODY GODDESS

Juicy Body Goddess owner Summer Lucille went TikTok viral with her catchphrase "You gotta be two-something to do something." She lives up to her sunny name and is the ultimate hype woman for her curvy clients. Plus-sized people travel from around the US to shop and experience Juicy Body Goddess's fun, welcoming environment.

From special-occasion looks to prom dresses to everyday casual outfits, the shop carries a range of stylish pieces in clothing sizes 10 to 32. If you want help curating your looks or one-on-one custom styling advice, you can also book a private consultation with Summer. The sessions are available for prom-dress shopping, bridal styling, and finding a sleek formal look. They also have one-on-ones for trans women who want to shop for their new style privately.

6801 Northlake Mall Dr., Ste. 237, 800-327-5020
juicybodygoddess.com

PROCURE THE PERFECT PRESENT
FROM PAPER SKYSCRAPER

Paper Skyscraper has been a hallmark of the Dilworth neighborhood for decades. Its sunny yellow awnings wave you in, and you're immediately met with a satisfying selection of cookbooks, local reads, popular paperbacks, and one of the best coffee-table book collections in the city.

The 5,000-square-foot shop has anything and everything you might want to gift, like luxury candles, kitschy kitchenware, personalized stationery, and pet toys. Around the holidays, I stock up on stocking stuffers like pocket-sized party games and interesting ornaments. My favorites are a golden yellow blown-glass reindeer balloon animal and one with the Charlotte skyline.

330 East Blvd., 704-333-7130
paperskyscraper.com

TIP

If you don't see a parking spot out front, enter off of Euclid Avenue where there are more spots around back and on the side.

95

TAP INTO YOUR CRAFT
AT CURIO, CRAFT & CONJURE

If you're interested in the mystical or are on a spiritual journey, this practical magic NoDa boutique is worth a visit. Climb up the creaky stairs, and you're shortly met with the aroma of incense, tables filled with crystals, bundles of herbs, cat candles, and other practical magic tools.

If you want to start building a ritual and don't know where to start, you can book a private consultation online. Someone will meet you at the store to share mantras, suggest tools, and anything else you might need. If you prefer to explore on your own time, they have a bounty of books around covering everything from crystals to chakras. If you're deeply curious and open to more, the shop also hosts a variety of workshops, from energy clearings to ancient history teachings. You can also book private tarot readings and events.

3204 N Davidson St., Ste. C, 980-207-0405
curiocharlotte.com

MEANDER
THROUGH ATHERTON MILL

The centerpiece of South End, Atherton is the neighborhood's shopping destination. It's home to chains like Lululemon, Sephora, West Elm, Warby Parker, and Anthropologie, along with local businesses. I'd start with an iced oat milk latte from Not Just Coffee to fuel your day of shopping, then stop at the Cocktailery, The beverage boutique was founded by Temu Curtis and is known for its interesting cocktail ingredients, creative classes, and beautiful barware.

Head to the Golden Carrot to marvel at its collection of contemporary fine jewelry. Pop into Uniquities where you'll find clothing brands from designers like Isabel Marant, Marie Oliver, FARM Rio, Loeffler Randall, and STAUD, before bopping over to Boem for more stylish selections. Bring home a bouquet from Bookout Blooms, or a bottle of wine from Vin Master.

2000–2140 South Blvd.
athertonsouthend.com

STROLL AROUND
SOUTHPARK MALL

The original crown jewel of the Queen City's shopping scene, SouthPark Mall has been around for more than half a century. The mall was cocreated by the Belk and Ivey families, and the iconic Southern department stores were its first anchors. SouthPark was initially a typical midpriced shopping destination but started to cater to luxury in the 2000s when Nordstrom and Neiman Marcus opened their doors. Its luxury status was cemented in 2012 when Gucci joined the retailer ranks. This new era of high-end shopping ushered in Louis Vuitton, Hermès, and Tiffany & Co. Today you can find a mix of designer showrooms, along with more accessible, contemporary tenants like Golden Goose, Aritzia, and Free People Movement. The mall is also home to one of Charlotte's oldest hidden gems, Arthur's, a sandwich shop and wine bar in Belk's basement.

4400 Sharon Rd.
simon.com/mall/southpark

PICK A PLANT
FROM OAKDALE GREENHOUSES

Whether you're a new plant parent or have a garden Martha Stewart would be jealous of, green thumbs of all levels will delight in the magic that is Oakdale Greenhouses. The plant-lovers paradise has one of the widest selections in the city, consisting of four greenhouses filled with flowers and indoor and outdoor plants. You can find a range of low-maintenance and experienced-plant-parent-only options and a mix of rare and common species. Don't let the size of the place overwhelm you; take time to enjoy its beauty and ask questions if needed. The staff knows their stuff and can help you find the right plant for your experience level and the space you want to put your new friend in.

5626 Statesville Rd., 704-596-4052
oakdalegreenhouses.com

TREAT YOURSELF TO A TREASURE
FROM TINY GODS JEWELRY STORE

I call homes that appear one way from the outside and another inside jewelry box houses. In Tiny Gods' case, the old Tudor-style cottage on Crescent Avenue is literally filled with jewels. Mary Margaret Beaver opened the fine jewelry shop in 2020, but this isn't your average stuffy showroom.

Tiny Gods is clad in rainbow rugs, locally made art, and funky gold light fixtures. The space itself is just as whimsical as the one-of-a-kind jewelry pieces on display. I've been lusting after their lollipop rings for a long, long time. The oversized, playful pieces typically feature a gemstone set in materials like opal, agate, or malachite. They sell a range of ready-to-wear earrings, necklaces, rings, and bracelets, and they do custom work, too. They also have in-house pop-up piercing events, if you need an excuse for another pair of earrings.

2325 Crescent Ave., 844-846-9463
tinygods.com

TIP

Looking for more treasures? Make an appointment with R.Runberg Curiosities, a hidden gem of a specialty home decor shop nearby. It's where you can find a Queen Charlotte bust candle in a rainbow of colors—a cool way to honor our city's namesake. Call 980-244-1042 to set an appointment.

100

BUY SOMETHING STYLISH AND SPECIAL
AT THIRTY-ONE JANE

Thirty-One Jane opened between the Elizabeth and Plaza Midwood neighborhoods back in 2022. But the seed was planted, maybe unknowingly at the time, more than 15 years ago when Susan Hamilton and Eloise Hamilton Reeves started taking mother-daughter trips to New York City, filled with shopping and flea-market hunting. They both had stints living in the West Village, too. All of that led to their first formal foray into fashion, opening Thirty-One Jane.

The trendy women's clothing boutique is designed to bring that West Village shopping experience to Charlotte, so you'll notice concrete floors, glowing chandeliers, and a comfy green sitting area. Thirty-One Jane carries brands like Proenza, Anine Bing, and Rachel Comey. You might find a cool pair of slouchy jeans, a crochet maxi dress, a structured cropped button-down, or colorful acrylic hoops—all elevated versions of effortlessly wearable silhouettes that you can wear again and again.

908 Pecan Ave., 980-202-0726
thirtyonejane.com

ACTIVITIES
BY SEASON

SPRING

Pick Your Produce from a Farmers Market, 88

Stroll through Rosie's Coffee & Wine Garden, 27

Make a Bouquet at McLawland Farms, 75

SUMMER

Paddle on the Catawba, 86

Let Live Music Move You, 52

Have One (or Two) Scoops from Two Scoops, 9

Play Pickleball at Rally, 70

FALL

Take the Kiddos to the Great Elizabeth Pumpkin Wall, 96

Get Your Adrenaline Pumping at Carowinds, 80

Get Cozy at Customshop, 40

Place Your Annual Baklava Sundae Order at the Greek Fest, 92

WINTER

Glide into the Holiday Spirit with Ice-Skating at the Whitewater Center, 78

Procure the Perfect Present from Paper Skyscraper, 122

Have a Classic Steak Dinner at Beef 'N Bottle, 22

SUGGESTED
ITINERARIES

DATE NIGHT

Cook Up Some Fun with Chef Alyssa, 108

Sip Mezcal from Puerta, 18

Enjoy a Show at the Comedy Zone, 53

OUTDOOR ENTHUSIASTS

Hike Crowders Mountain, 71

Make New Friends (and Get a Little Exercise) at Mad Miles Run Club, 72

Unleash Your Inner Adventurer at the US National Whitewater Center, 69

PATRON OF THE ARTS

Stroll through SOCO, 61

Catch a Concert at BofA, 54

Take a Self-Guided Mural Tour, 57

PARENTS AND FAMILY

Experience Afternoon Tea at Chez Marie Pâtisserie, 106

Discover Something New with the Family, 100

Celebrate Art at Charlotte SHOUT!, 58

SAVVY SHOPPERS

Get Lost in Sleepy Poet, 120

Riff through Records at Lunchbox, 51

Find Something Funky at Thrift Pony, 116

FOODIES

Do a Nonalcoholic Pairing at Restaurant Constance, 20

Taste Bites by Black Chefs, 98

Light Up All Five Senses at Counter-, 38

INDEX

704 Shop, 68
800 Degrees, 119
Abugida Ethiopian Cafe, 4
Al Mike's, 44
alice + olivia, 118
Amélie's French Bakery & Café, 11
Aqua e Vino, 3
Archive CLT, 97
Around the Crown 10K, 73
Aroy Thai, 13
Arthur's, 126
Asheville, NC, 25
Atherton Mill, 125
Babe & Butcher, 16
Baby Yoda and *Black Lives Matter* murals, 57
BackStage Lounge at SouthBound, 62
Bank of America Stadium, 54
Bao and Broth, 2, 6
Barcos Sports & Seafood, 59
Basil Thai, 12

Batch House, The, 10
BayHaven Food & Wine Festival, 98
Bechtler Museum of Modern Art, 90, 94
Beef 'n Bottle, 22
Belk Theater, 56
Birkdale Village, 81
Bitty & Beau's, 29
BlkMrktClt, 93
Blumenthal Performing Arts Center, 56
Boem, 125
Bojangles, xiv, 5
Bookout Blooms, 125
Booth Playhouse, 56
Botiwalla, 25
Boxcar Betty's, 6
Brakeman's Coffee & Supply, 88
Breakaway Festival, 52
Burial, 31
Burr & Berry Coffee, 29

Cabarrus Brewing Company, 59
Cafe Monte, 15
Calle Sol, 26
Camp North End, vi, 16, 46, 48, 50, 57, 79, 93
Cara's Cookie Company, 59
Carolina Panthers, 74
Carolina Renaissance Festival, 99
Carowinds, 80
Carowinds' WinterFest, 79
Carrigan Farms, 75
Catawba Nation Hand Carry Boat Launch, 86
Catawba River, 69, 86
Charleston, NC, 12, 82
Charlotte Checkers, 74
Charlotte FC, 42, 74
Charlotte Hornets, 74
Charlotte Knights, 74
Charlotte Latinx Pride, 104
Charlotte Pride Festival, 104
Charlotte Pride Interfaith Programs, 104
Charlotte Pride Parade, 104
Charlotte Regional Farmers Market, 89
Charlotte SHOUT!, 58
Charlotte Trans Pride, 104
Charlotte Women's Pride, 104
Chef Alyssa's Kitchen, 108
Chez Marie Pâtisserie, 106
Christmas Town U.S.A., 103
Churn Buddies, 59
Citrus Club, The, 82–83
Classic Attic, 120
Co-Op, The, 82–83
Coca-Cola 600, 74
Cocktailery, The, 125
Comedy Zone, 53
Common Market, The, 33
Confetti Hearts Wall, 57
Copain Bakery & Provisions, 29
Copper, 25
Cotswold Marketplace, 120
Counter-, 38
Counterculture Festival, 109
Crowders Mountain, 71
Curio, Craft & Conjure, 124
Curry Gate, 24

Customshop, 40
Daniel Stowe Botanical Garden, 87
Deejai Thai, 13
Depot at Gibson Mill, The, 59
Dilworth Tasting Room, 35
Discovery Place, 100–101
Discovery Place Kids, 100–101
Discovery Place Nature, 100–101
Discovery Place Science, 100–101
Dockside
Dumpling Lady, 6
Dupp & Swat, 50
EDIT Sale, 110, 114
El Puro Cuban Restaurant, 14
Elizabeth Park, 72
Enat, 6
Evening Muse, The, 55
Ever Andalo, 3
Extreme Ice Center, 78–79
Flower Child, 68
Four Mile Creek Greenway, 81
Free Range Brewing, 31
Freedom Park, 81
Gibbes Museum of Art, 82–83
Gibson Mill, 59
Gilde Brewery, 31
Golden Carrot, The, 125
Good Wurst Co., The, 68
Great Elizabeth Pumpkin Wall, 96
Green Brothers Juice and Smoothie Co., 76
Grow, 50
Haraz Coffee House, 29
Hardy Boys Records and Comics, 50
Harken, 82–83
Harvey B. Gantt Center for African-American Arts + Culture, 107
Heist Brewery, 31
Hex Coffee, Kitchen & Natural Wines, 46, 50
House of Nomad, 113
Hunnid Dollar Art Fair, 93
Jazzy Cheesecakes, 11
Jenni Kayne, 118
Johnny Roger's BBQ & Burgers, 59

JT Posh, 117
Juicy Body Goddess, 121
Kindred, 17
King of Spicy, 24
King Street, 82
Kings Drive Farmers Market, 89, 133
La Belle Helene, 56
La Caseta, 50
La Unica, 47
La Vie Style House, 118
Lake Wylie Dam Access Point, 86
Landsford Canal State Park, 86
Lang Van, 41
Leah & Louise, 7
Leatherman's, 85
Legion Brewing, 31
Leon's Fine Poultry & Oyster Shop, 82–83
Levine Center for the Arts, 56
Levine Museum of the New South, 107
Little Mama's, 3, 26
Little Sugar Creek Greenway, 81

Lovin' Life Music Fest, 52
Luck Factory Games, 59
LuLu's, 37
Lunchbox, 51
Lupitas Carniceria & Tortilleria, 47
Mac's Speed Shop, 62
Mad Miles Run Club, 72
Mama Ricotta's, 3, 26
Manolo's Latin Bakery, 11
Maria's, 47
Matthews Community Farmers' Market, 88
McDowell Creek Greenway, 81
McLawland Farms, 75
Mert's Heart and Soul, 32
Middle C Jazz, 65
Mint, The, 94
Mood House, 76
Music Yard, The, 62
NASCAR Hall of Fame, 74
Neighborhood Theatre, 64
Noble Smoke, 6
NoDa Brewing Company, 31
NoDa Company Store, 23

North Italia, 3
Not Just Coffee, 29, 61, 125
Oakdale Greenhouses, 127
Oggi, 3
Oh My Soul, 39
Olde Mecklenburg Brewery, The, 31
Optimist Hall, 6, 11, 25
Osteria Luca, 3
Ovens Auditorium, 56
Paddywax Candle Bar, 60
Palmetto Hotel, The, 82–83
Paper Skyscraper, 122
Papi Queso, 6
Park Road Books, 63
Park Road Shopping Center, 120
Pass, The, 82–83
Passage to India, 25
Pasta & Provisions, 34
Pauline Tea-Bar Apothecary, The, 36
Petra's, 64
Phillips Place, 118
Pilot Brewing, 31
Pineville Ice House, 78–79

Popbar, 50
Portofino's, 3
Protagonist Beer, 31
Puerta, 18
Puttery, 84
R.Runberg Curiosities, 129
Rail Trail, 68
Rally Pickleball, 70
Ralph Lauren, 118
Rat's Nest, The, 117
Reel Out Charlotte, 104
Reid's Fine Foods, 112
Reigning Donuts, 27
Resident Culture Brewing Company, 30
Restaurant Constance, 20
RH Rooftop Restaurant, 15
Rhino, 27
River Jam, 69
Riverwalk Rock Hill, 86
Rock Hill Outdoor Center at Riverwalk, 86
Room Service, 50
Rosie's Coffee & Wine Garden, 27
Rusty's Deli & Grille, 8

Salty Donut, 68
Salud Cerveceria, 42
SCarowinds, 80
Selenite, 68
Selwyn Avenue Pub, 21
Seven Oaks Nature Preserve, 87
Slate Interiors, 120
Sleepy Poet Antique Mall, 120
SOCO Gallery, 61
South End Exchange, 120
South End Farmers Market, 89
SouthBound, 62
Southern Christmas Show, 102
Southern Strain, 31
SouthPark Mall, 126
Stable Hand, 29
Stage Door Theater, 56
Stagioni, 2
Stash Pad, 117
Street Commerce, 117
Suárez Bakery, 11
Suffolk Punch, 31
Sullivan's Island, 82–83
Sumaq Coffee, 28
Superica, 47
Supperland, xvi, 45
Sycamore, 30
Tabor, 61
Tacos El Nevado, 47
Tacos el Regio, 47
Taylor Richards & Conger, 118
Team Rose Bread, 88
Thai House, 13
Thai Orchid, 13
Thai Taste, 13
Thirty-One Jane, 130
Thrift Pony, 116
Tiny Gods, 128
Trolley Barn Fermentory & Food Hall, 30
Truist Field, 79
Tuck Fest, 69
Two Scoops Creamery, 9
Underground, The, 55
Uptown Farmers Market, 57, 89
Uniquities, 125
US National Whitewater Center, 69

Vern's, 82–83
Veronet Vineyards, 71
Veronica Beard, 118
Vicente Bakery & Bistro, 11
Villani's Bakery, 11
Visulite Theatre, 55
Wells Fargo Championship, 77, 134
Wildroots Coffee, 29
Windy O'Connor Art + Home, 50
Wooden Robot Brewery, 30, 144
Yiasou Greek Festival, 92
Yunta, 43
YVY Training, 72
Zero George, 82–83

FROM CHARLOTTE WITH LOVE

@trashgenius @2gzandcountin

Mural outside of Wooden Robot Brewery by Garrison Gist (Paint Can Papi) and Rel Mariano (TrashGenius)